J✡urneys
to a
Jewish
Life

Inspiring Stories from
the Spiritual Journeys
of American Jews

J✡urneys
to a
Jewish
Life

Paula Amann

JEWISH LIGHTS Publishing
Woodstock, Vermont

Journeys to a Jewish Life:
Inspiring Stories from the Spiritual Journeys of American Jews

2007 First Printing
© 2007 by Paula Amann

Library of Congress Cataloging-in-Publication Data

Amann, Paula.
  Journeys to a Jewish life : inspiring stories from the spiritual journeys of American Jews / Paula Amann.
      p. cm.
  Includes bibliographical references.
  ISBN-13: 978-1-58023-317-0
  ISBN-10: 1-58023-317-1
  1. Spiritual life—Judaism. 2. Jewish way of life. 3. Jews—United States—Anecdotes. 4. Jews—United States—Identity. I. Title.
  BM723.A52 2007
  296.7092′2—dc22

                                                           2007034622

10   9   8   7   6   5   4   3   2   1

Manufactured in the United States of America
✿ Printed on recycled paper.
Jacket design: Jenny Buono

Published by Jewish Lights Publishing
A Division of Longhill Partners, Inc.
Sunset Farm Offices, Route 4, P.O. Box 237
Woodstock, VT 05091
Tel: (802) 457-4000   Fax: (802) 457-4004
www.jewishlights.com

Contents

Part II

Doors to the House

Part III

Dwelling Places

Acknowledgments

No book, especially one touching on spirituality, is written in a void. It takes family, friends, a community, publishing professionals, and a heaping spoonful of blind faith. A robust thank-you goes to Jewish Lights publisher Stuart M. Matlins, for believing in a rookie author's dream and helping to bring it to fruition. Applause, too, to Emily Wichland, for her patient guidance through all phases of the publishing process; to Jessica Swift, for her genuine enthusiasm and copyediting savvy; and all the other friendly, responsive staff at Jewish Lights, for never forgetting that writers are, first, human beings. My gratitude also goes to Arthur Magida, my book editor, for pinpointing the places that needed strengthening.

My hat's off to the other half of my writing support group, Mary Liepold, whose acute eye and exquisite ear for language improved the pages that follow. I look forward to her own book on bereaved parents who heal through activism and the arts.

Pamela Nadell, the Patrick Clendenen Professor of History and director of the Jewish Studies Program at American University in Washington, D.C., kindly reviewed rough drafts of several chapters. Jewish educator Norman Shore graciously read and commented on final versions of selected chapters. Rabbi Gerry Serotta and Hazzan Sunny Schnitzer also offered helpful feedback on individual chapters.

Thanks goes to friend extraordinaire Alan Amberg; Debra Kolodny, executive director of ALEPH: Alliance for Jewish Renewal; and Jewish Council for Public Affairs' Washington office director Hadar Susskind and Nigel Savage, director of

Hazon, for sharing multiple contacts. Rabbis Lia Bass, Carl Choper, Fred Scherlinder Dobb, Amy Eilberg, Ed Farber, David Krishef, Avis Miller, Robert Saks, Ethan Seidel, Gerry Serotta, Scott Sperling, Warren Stone, and Arthur Waskow all furnished helpful leads. Paul Bardack, Norma Brooks, Randy Herman, Barbara Israelite, and Beryl Michaels also supplied ideas that bore fruit. I also extend my appreciation to Dina April, Paul Bardack, Abby Bellows, April Berger, Bill Blocher, Sheila Fox, Rachel Kaplan, Amanda Milstein, Rabbi Dennis S. Ross, Reuven Walder, and Alan Wolfson for sharing their time and their stories.

Thank you to all the members of the Washington, D.C., *chavurah* (a Jewish worship group led by participants), where I make my spiritual home. Fabrangen's warmth, wisdom, and *heymish* (cozy) atmosphere is a gift to relative newcomers like me. Appreciation also goes to the staff of Kirsten's Cafe in Silver Spring, where hot tea and hearty soups fueled creation of much of this book.

Meanwhile, family members and friends, near and far, graciously tolerated rambling accounts of progress on the manuscript. Kudos to cousins Joe, who kindly commented on selected chapters, and Maria, who supplied computer first aid in a pinch. Also cheering from the sidelines were my father, Peter, and his wife, Jean, my brother, David, and my sister, Sandra, and Aunt Eva and Uncle Leo. Eva and my neighbor Kathy Morgan provided crucial babysitting in the home stretch of the book's first draft. My friend Joan Hyman offered timely encouragement. Danielita provided comic relief and a regular reminder that life, even on deadline, is replete with blessings. And long-distance runner Margo, my life partner, furnished unstinting moral and practical support over the entire length of this creative marathon.

Introduction

Isaac, a man so poor he goes to bed hungry, dreams of finding a buried treasure under a bridge near the royal palace. He follows his vision, sometimes hitching wagon rides, but mostly walking for days, over hills and through deep valleys, to the big city.

Finding the bridge he pictured in his dreams, he discovers that it is guarded by soldiers. The captain of the guards laughs at his quest, saying he himself has dreamed of digging up a fortune under the stove of a man named Isaac. The poor traveler trudges the long road home, only to find enough wealth to sustain him for a lifetime, just where the captain described it.

Isaac ends up finding close at hand the riches that he'd sought in a faraway place. This story from the Hasidic tradition, one of Judaism's mystical strains—found in Martin Buber's *The Way of Man* and retold by Uri Shulevitz in his luminous children's classic, *The Treasure*—captures the essence of the real-life vignettes you are about to read.

As these stories document, a significant number of Jews have set forth on a life-changing quest. Observers have chronicled the *ba'al teshuvah* (return to Orthodoxy) movement that has drawn an estimated hundreds of thousands into the traditional Jewish world. Yet the quiet return of secular and liberal Jews to a more eclectic, yet equally committed Judaism has taken place largely out of the limelight.

In recent years, many American Jews have stumbled upon spiritual wealth in the heart of their own tradition. Often traveling paths as roundabout as Isaac's, they have wandered far in search of a spiritual life that feeds their soul, only to discover it in their own heritage. Many belong to the baby boomer generation, born largely to parents intent on assimilation and the sheer struggle for survival. Others are much older or considerably younger than the boomers. They live in cities, suburban tracts, and rural corners of the United States, but they share a similar quest. While they may work as nurses and lawyers, entrepreneurs and artists, teachers and social justice activists, they all seek to infuse their lives with a spirituality grounded in Judaism. In their own ways, at their own pace, these twenty-first-century pilgrims are blazing trails of renewal to a Jewish life that draws on the past, stands in the present, and looks firmly forward.

I approach this trend, the return of Jewish seekers to the religiously liberal streams of Judaism, not as a scholar or a rabbi, but as a journalist. My job, as I see it, is to chronicle some of the stories of the people who are rediscovering their Jewish heritage and let their voices ring, drawing a few of my own conclusions along the way. The book's structure is designed to mirror some of the stages of their spiritual odysseys. "Homeward," the first part, explores milestones on the Jewish journey, from inspiration, to alienation, to finding community, and living with contradictions. The second part, "Doors to the House," examines several portals into Judaism, from family ties, to the Jewish arts scene, to the inadvertent but often profound effects of confronting illness and personal loss. In the third and final portion of the book, "Dwelling Places," I spend some time visiting the destinations of today's Jewish journeys, from encounters with God to personal rituals. I also suggest some lessons from these spiritual explorations, both for the Jewish community and for individual seekers.

Some of the opinions of those interviewed are at odds with the stands of mainstream religious and communal organizations. Yet I believe the remarks of these returning Jews are worth hearing whether or not they may be shared by a majority of Jews in the pews and leadership roles. The voices of Jews who have stood on the margins of our community can shed light on where our religious institutions need to grow and change. In that spirit, I have included a chapter, "Pathless in the Promised Land," on emerging terrain in the Jewish world—from the environmental movement, to spiritual direction, to yoga—that is generating enthusiasm among many Jewish seekers. As I suggest there, time and religious trial and error will govern whether some of the new developments in Judaism will persist, or whether they will give way to other innovations we have yet to imagine.

Let me introduce you to a couple of the people you will meet in *Journeys to a Jewish Life*. Biochemist-turned-author Maggie Anton, fifty-seven, says she took up the study of the Talmud, the voluminous written version of Judaism's postbiblical oral law, to keep pace with the studies of her husband, who had just begun learning Hebrew. Delving into these texts has taken this secular-bred Californian on an absorbing and unpredictable trip into a faith she once thought she didn't need.

In fact, Anton's explorations of Rashi, the renowned eleventh-century Talmudist, led her to re-create the lives of his learned daughters in the trilogy of novels *Rashi's Daughters*. "I think of myself as being on the *Rashi's Daughters* escalator," Anton said. "I can't get off, I can't turn around and get back, and I'm not sure where it's going." But she seems eager to continue the ride, wherever it leads. "So far," Anton said, "it's been a great journey."

Jeffrey Lash, a manufacturer's representative in New York's Hudson River Valley, grew up a Conservative Jew, but ditched religion when he graduated from high school and joined the Navy. He had experienced his bar mitzvah as a soulless "process that was done to me" and barely stepped into a synagogue for some thirty years. Then, at fifty-two, Lash and his wife, Sandra, joined Congregation Shir Chadash of the Hudson Valley, a Reform synagogue in Poughkeepsie, New York, as a way to bring community into their lives. They gained that, and more. Their involvement led them into such social action projects as helping to rebuild arson-damaged African American churches in the South. For Lash, the experience underscored a core religious teaching: "To be Jewish, you have to do."

Now sixty-five and a past president of his temple, Lash takes part in Torah study twice a month with a diverse group of other Jewish seekers. "Sitting around the table, you get the doctor, the cop, and the college professor," Lash said. "We're all on a journey. We're on the same train, but we're getting on and off at different times."

Lash and Anton are among the over sixty people I interviewed in the course of writing this book. They belong to congregations in many streams of Judaism—Reform, Conservative, Reconstructionist, Renewal, and the *chavurah* movement—but they share the outlook of the seeker for whom questions of faith matter as much as answers.

With renewed interest in spirituality and heightened worries about Jewish continuity, the time is ripe for a book that explores the return of secular Jews to a wide spectrum of deeply felt religious practice. The Judaica shelves of major bookstores offer many guides to Jewish observance to tutor the novice or refresh the knowledge of the returnee. Yet few works explore the ups, downs, and meanders of the spiritual quest from the viewpoint of Jews who have actually undertaken it.

A few of the people I have profiled in *Journeys to a Jewish Life* bear well-known names. Most, by design, do not. The road home to a Jewish life is open to all, and some of the most humble seekers have the most amazing stories to tell. Spirituality, like everything in a culture dominated by market values, often comes wrapped in commercial hype, neat formulas for self-improvement, and a one-size-fits-all approach more appropriate for cheap socks than the infinite variety of religious experience. In the interests of authenticity, you will hear the words of the people I interviewed in as close to their unvarnished form as grace of expression and grammar will allow.

Driving my enthusiasm for this project is my own winding road home from an intellectually and culturally rich, but thoroughly secular, childhood to nearly a decade of work in the Jewish press and communal world. For more than seven years, I was news editor for the *Washington Jewish Week*. Before that, I was a staff writer at B'nai B'rith International. *Journeys to a Jewish Life* draws inspiration from many of the people I met during my career as a journalist. Their spiritual explorations, a few of which appear in this book, continue to provide me with food for reflection and wonder.

My own religious wanderings began in my teen years in the Detroit area, where I immersed myself in the Judaica section of the public library. The Holocaust, which drove my father, an aunt, and my grandparents out of Europe in 1941, loomed as a shadow over my childhood, even as I yearned to know more about my rather assimilated Jewish heritage. Indeed, I came from a family where, in the Old Country (Austria-Hungary), my forebears had softened the ethnic overtones of their names, changing "Amschelberger" to "Amann," "Israel" to "Iranyi." Yet something shifted in my psyche when my beloved Grandma Dora, an exuberant refugee from Vienna, gave me a record of Yiddish songs. Somehow, these melodies I had never heard before touched me like the voice of an old friend.

Like many in my boomer generation, I delved into the teachings of Eastern religions during my college years. Later I flirted with, but never quite committed myself to, Quakerism. Then, some two decades ago, I sat down at a women's Passover seder in Chicago and experienced the Exodus in miniature.

The liberation themes of the Haggadah, an updated, gender-inclusive version of the traditional script, connected with the worldly values of social justice I held dear. I was hooked.

I walked into Judaism through the portal of the *chavurah* movement, with its participatory worship style. Ill at ease with the foreign sounds of Hebrew prayer, I was also clueless in some ways about what this religion had to say about dealing with other people. Joining the Jewish Reconstructionist Congregation in Evanston, Illinois, widened my Jewish horizons. There, through Cantor Lori Lippitz, I encountered the klezmer revival, and sang with her synagogue band, Heavy Shtetl. My Jewish path since then has led me to Reconstructionist, Reform, and lay-led *chavurah*-style congregations in the Washington, D.C., area, where I make my home. I do not claim to have arrived at a final destination on my Jewish adventure, though I hope it has refined some of the rougher edges of my character, a lifelong project.

All of the people whose spiritual safaris are told in *Journeys to a Jewish Life* have spent years searching for a meaningful spirituality, sometimes at odds with their secular or conventional Jewish backgrounds. No two people take the same journey—each unfolds at a different rhythm, with a singular set of twists and turns, valleys and peaks. Yet the telling of each story can ease the footsteps of those who follow.

Think of these people—these pilgrims—as traveling companions on whatever Jewish journey you may be taking or considering. It is my hope that their tales will offer you camaraderie, a guidepost here and there, and most of all, the heart and strength to pursue your own path. No one has an exclusive claim on clarity or wisdom. Each of us is capable of discovering nuggets of truth and insight along our way. Together, each from our own corner of darkness and light, we take the next step on the road home to a Jewish life.

I

Homeward

1 Kindling Flames
Coming Full Circle

Connie Songer found her Jewish soul in a family tree. The genealogical chart prepared for a cousin's bar mitzvah jolted the Methodist-raised woman into a revelation: she and her six siblings sprang from Cohens and Levys—not Clarks and Larkins, as name changes in her parents' generation had led her to believe. The Mechanicsburg, Pennsylvania, nurse practitioner, who was then in her late thirties and regularly attending Quaker meeting, recalls gazing into a mirror shortly after that new knowledge rocked her world.

"Nothing had changed, and everything had changed," said Songer, a warm and articulate mother of two, now fifty-nine. "I looked into my eyes and thought, 'I'm another woman.'" It took nine months of reading about Jewish history, religion, and culture—plus catch-up conversations with family members—before she spoke with a rabbi. Another nine months flew by before she stepped into a synagogue to hear the rhythms of Hebrew prayer for the first time in her life. "The first service I went to, I knew I'd found where I belonged spiritually," Songer said. "I felt I'd come home."

Listen to stories from Jewish communities across the United States and you will hear of many such homecomings—though not all are as dramatic as Songer's, whose midlife discovery spurred her to reclaim her Jewish roots. Yet, at the start of each of these stories is a spark that kindles a Jewish flame. It can take the form of the spoken or written word, an encounter with another soul, the birth of a child, an artistic creation, or an act of communal service that touches off a blaze of insight, hope, and change.

Indeed, later chapters will examine the spiritual doors opened by mentors, family, the arts, and social justice movements, to name a few portals into Jewish life. And early chapters will track some of the milestones, twists, and obstacles common to many journeys on the road home to Judaism. But for the moment, let us take a *tour d'horizon*, a quick overflight above the landscape of Jewish spirituality as it is unfolding in the United States today.

Giving Faith a Fresh Look

People raised nonreligious or nominally Jewish are giving their heritage another chance in adulthood, sometimes as they become parents and wonder what to teach their children about moral values. Confronting the death of a parent, marital upheaval, career shifts, and other personal challenges can also open the heart and provoke existential questions. A Jewish dropout in his early adult years, Jeffrey Kahn, fifty-seven, hadn't given his heritage much thought since the lavish "parental party" that was his bar mitzvah. "Judaism was just a generational tie for me," said Kahn, owner of the Unicorn gift shop in Woodstock, Vermont. "It was having children that changed that for me."

As he grappled with choices over the religious education of his kids some two decades ago, Kahn says he realized he wanted them to have a Jewish upbringing, but one different than his own. Raised Reform in a New Jersey suburb of New York City, this entrepreneur recalls going through religious rituals without learning any context that would give them personal meaning. "I was forced to be bar mitzvahed, and there was nothing spiritual about it," said Kahn.

Yet Kahn's commitment to his family put this once-alienated Jew onto a path of congregational life as a member of Congregation Shir Shalom, the Woodstock Area Jewish Community. Reclaiming "a living link" to Judaism, said Kahn, took finding the right congregation where he could grow spiritually alongside his children. "Now I see my kids and other kids experiencing what being Jewish is," he said, citing the sense of normalcy they gained through being part of a synagogue in their largely Christian New England town.

Jews on their road home also say that the right words at the right time, coming from a trusted or a spiritually potent source, can reroute whole lives in the direction of Jewish practice. Secular-bred Joanne Doades, now curriculum development director in the department of lifelong learning at the Union for Reform Judaism and author of *Parenting Jewish Teens: A Guide for the Perplexed* (Jewish Lights), grew up with little grasp of her heritage. "I did not know that Saturday was the Jewish Sabbath until I was in my early thirties," admitted Doades, who now has grown children. Attending High Holy Day services during her first year of marriage with her then non-Jewish husband (who has since become a Jew by choice), she recalls feeling "very embarrassed and uncomfortable." Jewish practice seemed a foreign culture to her.

Doades' tensions began melting away when her husband voiced appreciation at his first exposure to Judaism's holiest days, Yom Kippur and Rosh Hashanah. In the churches that he knew, he told her, the attention seemed to be on death. At synagogue, in contrast, life took stage center. "That was like a thunderbolt to me," said Doades of his remark. "I was so struck by an outside observer looking at what I had ignored for so long and finding it important and beautiful." This would lead her to reexamine her Jewish roots and help other young parents create the kind of Jewish home she herself was building.

The right trip to Israel at the right time has forged a link to religious heritage for some disconnected Jews. Filmmaker Erik Greenberg Anjou—for whom striving to excel in prep school had supplanted Judaism after his bar mitzvah—got a taste of the Jewish state in his late thirties through a study tour. He has yearned to live there part-time ever since. "I was on fire the whole time," Anjou said. "There's a land where you belong and it's not necessarily the land where you were born." He went on to make the award-winning 2006 documentary *A Cantor's Tale*, which depicts the triumphs and travails of Brooklyn-born Cantor Jacob Mendelson, a man bent on preserving traditional cantorial singing. Anjou, a self-styled spiritual "mutt" who has moonlighted as a cantor, has come to find meaning in both Conservative and Orthodox Jewish worship.

Down Other Roads and Back

Exposure to the Holocaust precipitates, for some Jews, a period of soul-searching and a resolve to assert the religious identity that the Nazis ruthlessly tried to eradicate. A searing encounter with this history led photographer Lloyd Wolf, coauthor of *Jewish Mothers: Strength, Wisdom, Compassion* and *Jewish Fathers: A Legacy of Love* (Jewish Lights), to rekindle the lights of his own Judaism. Hired to take pictures for the 1990 March of the Living, which took American teens from the former death camps of Europe to modern-day Israel, Wolf had his own adult rite of passage along the way. "It overpowered me like a tsunami," recalled Wolf, now fifty-five and living in Arlington, Virginia. "I realized that the Holocaust was like an ocean of murder and this was my people."

Stirred by the sight of a mound of human ashes at the Maidanek concentration camp, he first recited a prayer from the Native American tradition, one of many spiritual disciplines he had explored. It was an invocation to the water spirits that he had learned from the singing of the 1970s folk rock duo, Brewer and Shipley. "Then I switched to *Kaddish* and never went back," said Wolf, citing the Jewish mourner's prayer, which extols the greatness of God in the face of personal loss. "It was mine. I didn't have to do any translation, though I don't speak Aramaic." With other participants, he cobbled together an impromptu *Yizkor* (memorial) service at the camp. It was the beginning of Wolf's own personal march to a meaningful Jewish practice, which in time would lead him to the Fabrangen *chavurah*, a lay-led congregation in Washington, D.C.

Some spiritual seekers, after exploring other faith traditions, are drawn back to Judaism and are surprised to find sustenance they had never tasted in Hebrew school. It took Deborah Oleshansky, forty-five, journeys into Hindu-based meditation and Native American healing rituals before she was able to recapture the "incredible combination of strength and joy" she sensed as a girl while celebrating Shabbat with her maternal grandmother. Synagogue life felt devoid of spirituality, and for some years as an adult, she sought wisdom in other disciplines. Jewish Renewal teachers at the Elat Chayyim Center for Jewish Spirituality, then in upstate New York, eventually helped her find the depth in her own religion. "When I make a blessing now before I eat ... I really feel something when I say the words," said Oleshansky, a domestic violence activist turned Jewish educator in Knoxville, Tennessee. "Saying the words is calling in a bigger presence."

The simple act of voicing gratitude for bread puts her in touch with God.

Many Doors to the House

Jewish spiritual travelers include those drawn to communal roles—rabbis, cantors, educators like Oleshansky—after half a lifetime in the secular world.

Others have found a vocation in the Jewish arts, from calligraphy to woodwork, and from dance to theater. Count among those New York trumpeter Frank London, a key figure in such ensembles as the Klezmatics, who reclaimed a deeper Jewish selfhood as he explored the ecstasy of Hasidic music. Raised Reform on Long Island, he recalls a boyhood in which Jewish ritual practices played only minor roles, as was common in the Reform movement of the 1960s and 70s: "I don't think I heard the word *kosher* [referring to preparing food according to Jewish dietary laws] until I was in synagogue." But the Hasidic approach rekindled his interest in Judaism. "The whole idea is that God can be reached through joy ... singing, dancing," said London, forty-nine.

Some Jews find their niche in efforts to promote social justice in the broader world. That passion has fueled the life of New York–born Margie Klein, twenty-eight. Educated at the city's Abraham J. Heschel School, a Jewish day school, Klein does not strictly fit the profile of a once alienated Jew. Yet she says she has drawn much of the inspiration for her spirituality from Christian social justice activists. Following a successful drive for a ballot initiative in the late 1990s to provide affordable housing and support services to homeless women in New Haven, Connecticut, Klein, then a student at Yale, had her first adult glimpse of powering social change with the energy of faith.

"That was a religious turning point," said Klein, who canvassed for the measure. "It really felt to me like a miracle ... that this whole group of people, which came from such different backgrounds, were able to bridge our boundaries to work together for a common vision." The experience, she says, reframed her understanding of "the idea of oneness in Judaism" as "the way the world is connected when we live out our values." Klein is now pursuing rabbinical studies at the Rabbinical School of Hebrew College in Newton Centre, near Boston.

The current generation of seekers encompasses those who are creating new paradigms, using spiritual direction, environmental activism, or yoga to enhance Jewish life. Judith Dack, of Bethesda, Maryland, was once a disaffected Sephardic Jew. Her religious development stalled in childhood, amid her grandmother's stringent "don'ts" list for Shabbat observance. Paradoxically, Dack rediscovered her faith after training as a yoga teacher. The experience opened her heart to spirituality. "It was getting into the world of ritual, sanctity, looking beyond this world for support," Dack explained. "Before that, the 'God word' was an instantaneous shutdown." Now, as she offers yoga and chanting classes infused with Judaism, she sees herself as an informal outreach worker to Jews who are as alienated from their heritage as she once was.

Since its inception, the Jewish experience has revolved around the laws and stories of the Torah, or five biblical books of Moses; generations of rabbinic interpretation collected in the Talmud; and discussion about both that inspires other books to this day. Given this heritage, it should not startle anyone that some twenty-first-century seekers find their spiritual moorings in the printed word. In Alexandria, Virginia, human resources consultant David Blumenstein, forty-four, found his way back to Jewish life after trying other spiritual paths, including Buddhism and several personal growth movements. At eighteen, he lost his beloved grandmother to a brain tumor and, in his rage at her death, rejected Judaism. "I remember feeling God doesn't listen to prayer: My grandmother died and this isn't supposed to happen," Blumenstein recalled. "At that point, I turned a switch off."

Thirteen years later in a New York bookshop, a family friend handed him Lawrence Kushner's *The River of Light: Jewish Mystical Awareness* (Jewish Lights), and in its pages, Blumenstein found a kindred spirit. The mystical writings of Kushner and also of Abraham Joshua Heschel, he discovered, offered a Jewish perspective that spoke to his deepest yearnings. "There was a way in Judaism to connect with all the things that I'd been searching for," Blumenstein said. Esoteric knowledge, he now believes, is "hidden in plain sight," in such practices as the observance of Shabbat, when Jews halt their week's labors to better savor relationships with family, friends, and God.

From the pages of books, Blumenstein eventually moved to the pews of Alexandria's Conservative Agudas Achim Congregation. Yet, like many profiled here, he moves in more than one stream of Judaism. He is also a board member of ALEPH: Alliance for Jewish Renewal, the institutional arm of the Jewish Renewal movement. "Spirituality is like the ocean," Blumenstein said. "All we're doing when we follow our religious forms is dipping our cup in the ocean. This tradition, that's the cup I want to drink from."

As for Connie Songer—the nurse whose story opens this chapter—she would move from her first, strangely comfortable Jewish service to joining a teen confirmation class. It jump-started the religious education she'd never had. "There was this strong sense of my mind and my soul finding a meeting place, the intellectual and the spiritual coming together," said Songer of her early encounters with Judaism. While reclaiming her religious roots over the past dozen years, Songer has risen to leadership in her Reconstructionist synagogue, serving on the board and eventually as its president.

Her life today, she says, moves to the rhythms of the Jewish calendar. In fact, when I interviewed her, she was busy observing Passover. "Years ago, we would have been buying Easter baskets with jelly beans, and coloring eggs," reflected Songer. "That feels foreign now." Now earning a master's degree in Jewish history at Baltimore Hebrew University, Songer relishes the opportunity to broaden her knowledge and keep growing into her rediscovered faith. "It's endless learning," Songer said. "There is a seeking in Judaism that takes you closer and closer to God. There's no way you can get too close."

The kind of journey she is describing takes American Jews over diverse terrain, on varied routes. As we will see, some find obstacles on the road into Judaism that spill them onto other spiritual paths—or drive them out of spiritual life altogether. Some gain a momentum from their early moves toward reclaiming a Jewish life that propels them forward. For many, finding guides, or mentors, eases the journey. A sizeable number, meanwhile, hang back at the gates of the Jewish community, distanced by their ignorance of Hebrew, ritual, and the wealth of unwritten customs that can overwhelm the returning Jew. After a time, most who continue on the journey search out a congregation where they can hang their hat and find traveling companions. And over the long haul, even the most ardent seekers take issue with parts of Judaism, even as they come to call it their own.

These spiritual adventure stories will take us from life's sheerest peaks to its deepest valleys and back again. We will track the progress and pitfalls of American Jews on their roads home as they explore the meaning of their heritage. A businesswoman rediscovers her faith as she battles cancer. A psychologist follows his spiritually precocious daughter back into the synagogue. A biochemist encounters God's presence, incongruously, at her gym. A labor activist from the former Soviet Union walks into Judaism through the door marked "justice." Throughout these journeys to a Jewish life, ordinary people at extraordinary moments, as in any human enterprise, falter and start again, follow few straight lines, and end up at unexpected destinations.

Yet too many people on the spiritual quest still struggle to find a nourishing sense of intimacy with the Divine or even a durable Jewish community. In the chapter that follows, we will explore some of the roots of religious disenchantment.

2
Lost on the Way to Sinai
Wandering Off a Jewish Path

Philadelphia's Melvin Metelits, seventy-four, turned toward the exit door from Jewish life at his own bar mitzvah. Just before the ceremony, his rabbi called Metelits into his office to ask whether he planned to continue studying Judaism. Out of his concern for his working-class family's tight budget—and his own passion for baseball—the boy said he would not. After hearing this, the rabbi erupted in the middle of the ceremony.

"From the pulpit, during his sermon, he launched into a blistering attack on parents who don't encourage their children to continue their Jewish studies and called them 'dried up twigs on the glorious tree of Judaism,'" said Metelits, who recalled turning red-faced with anger and embarrassment on the *bimah* (altar). "It's sixty years ago, and I still remember." He continued going to services for one more year before quitting synagogues altogether for close to five decades. "There was no spirituality in my Jewish education," said Metelits, speaking in a husky, impassioned whisper in the wake of throat surgery.

13

Talk to American Jewry's former expatriates and you'll find more disappointed lovers than harsh critics of religion. For many of them, the face of Judaism—family, clergy, a teacher, or even an entire congregation—fell critically short of its touted ideals. At a critical moment, someone's hypocritical pronouncement, cold judgment, or rigid insistence on tradition over compassion trumped the justice, the lovingkindness, and the essential sense of welcome that is at the heart of Jewish heritage.

Many disenchanted Jews, like foiled romantics, are also hungering for more meaningful relationships with something greater than themselves, something more than they actually discerned in congregational life. Synagogues may begin as idealistic enterprises, they suggest, but too often come to revolve around dues rather than divinity, internal politics rather than a transcendent community.

In the case of Metelits, the rabbi whose outburst had left him blushing on the *bimah* during his bar mitzvah would drive his former student out of Judaism for most of a lifetime. That same spiritual leader made what Metelits called a "vitriolic" appeal for funds on the next Yom Kippur, reading aloud the names of families in the congregation whom the rabbi believed were capable of contributing more. "I walked out and never went back for forty-seven years," said Metelits, who abandoned Jewish life for nearly five decades as a "comrade" in the Communist Party.

Outsiders in Jewish Life

Jewish seekers long for a sense of communal embrace, of welcome that too often seems unevenly extended. Sadly, some religious institutions have a spotty record of responding to women clergy and other leaders, working-class Jews, gays and lesbians, people with disabilities, singles, and others who feel like outsiders for various reasons.

Shafir "Candy" Lobb dates her long disillusion with Judaism to being rebuffed in an Ohio synagogue. As this rabbi's daughter tells the story, she walked into the sanctuary in 1979 wrapped in a *tallit*, the prayer shawl that women in liberal Jewish denominations had begun reclaiming. Her entrance precipitated an exodus of several leaders of the Conservative congregation, starting with one of the rabbis. After about ten men marched out, Lobb departed not only from that house of worship, but also from the organized Jewish community for close to twenty years. "I drifted and became largely secular," she said. She built an engineering career in product design and evaluation at the Goodyear Tire and Rubber Company and put her religious identity on hold. "I wore my Jewish jewelry inside my shirt," said Lobb, who stopped taking time off for Jewish holidays.

Not until her mother died in 1998 did Lobb venture back into a synagogue or two—including the Conservative congregation that had turned its collective back on her—to say *Kaddish*. The bereaved woman and her prayer shawl experienced a distinctly different reception. This time, "They offered me an *aliyah* [blessing before the reading of Torah]," Lobb said. "On the way out, one of the *tzitzit* [knotted fringes] of my *tallit* broke and the cantor offered me a new *tallit*."

She returned the next week and later took part in a sisterhood conference, witnessing the gender equality that had swept the Jewish world over the previous two decades, in tandem with the growing ordination of women rabbis. "Then I realized that women were playing a much bigger role," said Lobb. "They were fully participating in the service; there was no distinction anymore, which was the dream I'd always had." Six months after her mother's death, Lobb was exploring her own dream deferred: studying to become a rabbi. She now leads a Reform-style congregation in Tucson, Arizona.

Education That Fails

Ironically, for many in the baby boomer generation and older, Jewish religious education proved a stumbling block on the road to a spiritual life. Growing up as Paul Rheingold in the New York borough of Queens, Pinchas Zohav attended a modern Orthodox religious school that did not quench his thirst for wisdom. "I've always been a spiritual person, but I wasn't fed in that environment," said Zohav, fifty-seven, now of Seattle. "I always had a hunger for something, but I was totally starved when I got out of Talmud Torah."

His education represented a compromise between his secular parents, who had been born in Brooklyn, and a more observant older generation from what is now the western part of the Ukraine. Zohav was close to his maternal grandfather, who went to Shabbat evening prayers near his home in the Bronx, but Zohav's parents largely shunned Judaism. "I don't remember either one of them ever using the word *God*," said Zohav. "They were so busy assimilating to this country."

Yet the traditional faith that Zohav encountered at the Talmud Torah, where he studied two or three days a week, created culture shock as he bounced between religious and secular worlds. "It was as if my Jewish identity existed between the Bronx and the Talmud Torah, with a piece of nothing in between, which was my home," said Zohav. And, as he grew to think for himself, he spurned what he saw as the "irrelevant, if not oppressive, content" he had learned in religious school.

The Zionist movement captured his imagination. "I found it a wonderful solution to my problems," he said, since it showed "how to be Jewish without being religious." At twenty-three, Zohav moved to Israel. He lived there for five years, married, and Hebraicized his original name. "Had I grown up in a different environment, I would have been a rabbi," said Zohav, now an ordained Jewish Renewal rabbinic pastor and freelance chaplain. "Between the existential challenge of growing up in the post-Holocaust world and the lack of spiritual resource in my family's home, the thought of pursuing religious studies never arose." His inward journey would remain in the secular realm until a positive encounter with the Jewish Renewal movement some two decades later brought him to a more traditional religious spirituality.

For many more Jews than Metelits, the bar and bat mitzvah has been failing its larger purpose as a doorway to adult Jewish commitment. Kids are quick to spot the contradictions between the Jewish values they have been taught and a ceremony that feels perfunctory, bereft of meaning, or overshadowed by the party afterward.

Rebecca Spilke, raised a Conservative Jew in Poughkeepsie, New York, recalls a minimalist celebration of her coming-of-age with a cake in the family backyard. The party was a metaphor: being a Jew was more of a spiritual dessert than a main course. Hebrew school, with its rote memorization of vocabulary, had left her cold. "The highlights were the ten-minute breaks when you could get French fries," said Spilke, now thirty-two and living in Queens, New York. "It was a frontal lecture and there was no connection made by our teachers between what we were learning and anything else in our lives." She dropped off the Jewish map for a dozen years after her bat mitzvah.

In adulthood, curiosity about the Jewish roots of which she knew so little led Spilke to a three-year stay in Israel. That experience, in turn, drew her into serious religious practice, including observing Shabbat and keeping kosher. Resettled in Queens, she recently helped launch a minyan that melds a traditional approach, including a *mechitzah* (a partition between men and women), with services led by both genders. "I strive to walk the balance between the way I was brought up, which was to see Judaism as the pursuit of social justice and activism" while "keeping as much of a Halachic life [in accordance with Jewish law] as I can," Spilke said.

Richard Chused, sixty-four, grew up in a "seriously Reform" congregation in St. Louis, Missouri, which had taken the movement's historic rejection of Jewish tradition to such an extreme that some services were held on Sunday. "A *kippah* [skullcap worn by men and some women in Jewish settings] was outlawed and nobody wore a *tallit*; that was just out of the question," Chused recalled. The temple was so bent on distancing itself from the past that it didn't even offer boys the option of a bar mitzvah ceremony. What religious education it did provide left Chused uninspired. "I really loathed it," he said of Hebrew school. "I exited that place finding very little of value in it." He would go on to college and attend one reception at the campus Hillel center. No one spoke a word to him and he never returned. "That was that, for many years," said Chused of his Jewish disenchantment.

Chused became a staunch atheist. He made the transition from rationalist to awe-struck Jew some dozen years ago. As he and his wife, Elizabeth, were considering Jewish education for one of their sons, they happened to hear a *drash* (short sermon) by Rabbi Avis Miller at Adas Israel Congregation, a Conservative synagogue in Washington, D.C. Chused can't remember the Torah portion that day, but he still recalls the impact of a religious leader who conveyed both intellectual depth and passionate belief. "It blew us both away," he recalled. For Chused, the rabbi's words—"full of wonderful stories and history ... angst and emotion and power"—began to weave what would become for him an enduring connection between the life of the mind and that of the soul. Now a law professor at Georgetown University, he follows the rhythms of a work-free Shabbat and has affixed a *mezuzah* beside his office door.

Across the Jewish spectrum, Judaism's emphasis on deeds over dogma leaves some, especially those with a thin or nonexistent religious education, baffled and estranged. Too often, say Jews who drift away, the practices of their faith—from

Shabbat observance, to the yearly round of holidays, to the kosher laws—were presented stripped of heart and ethics.

For much of his life, Miami lawyer David Abraham didn't find Judaism wrapped in any meaningful context until he gave it another chance in his early forties. He grew up in a Cleveland family that practiced little Judaism. "All they ever did was Chanukah candles and presents, and as quick a Passover seder as you could get away with," recalled Abraham, now forty-seven. Sensing that he knew little of his heritage, he spent two fruitless years in a Conservative religious school after his bar mitzvah.

While studying at the University of South Florida, he was smitten with an Italian Catholic woman, yet he ultimately bowed to the Jewish tradition of avoiding marriage outside the faith and did not wed her—a source of some bitterness. "I hated God for that," Abraham said. "I saw religion as a way of keeping people apart." A trip to Israel at twenty-two during law school forged a lasting loyalty to the Jewish state, but it failed to offer him the spirituality he sought. "It's not enough to connect with Israel or say you're Jewish," Abraham said. "It was never enough for me. I couldn't seem to find a way in."

Yet his distance from his Jewish roots did not bring him any closer to Christianity, which he blamed for much of the persecution Jews had endured in the Diaspora, from the Crusades through the Holocaust. "I was really turned off by what religion had done," Abraham said. Once married to a Jewish woman, he and his wife raised their children Jewish, which left the door ajar to future explorations when Abraham was ready to walk through it.

For most women who grew up in the first half of the twentieth century, a full Jewish education—not to mention a career as a rabbi or cantor—lay out of reach. Most religious instruction was aimed at boys, who studied in preparation for their bar mitzvah ceremony. The bat mitzvah for girls remained

the exception until the 1960s, when this coming-of-age ceremony spread like lilies of the valley, first in the Conservative
movement, then among Reform Jews, after its 1922 U.S. debut
with Judith Kaplan, the daughter of Mordechai Kaplan,
founder of Reconstructionist Judaism.

Though both her brothers celebrated their bar mitzvah,
Judith B. Edelstein had little religious education growing up in
Brooklyn, New York, though she recalls being "the star of the
singing teacher" at the secular Yiddish school she briefly
attended. Yet, Edelstein, who would become a rabbi in her forties, feels that she imbibed Jewish values of caring for the poor
by watching her mother's actions. The house was full of
tzedakah boxes (literally, "justice boxes," which are used to col-
lect money for worthy causes). Edelstein remembers her
mother balancing the family's material wants with the obligation to give to those around her. "She was the first one in the
neighborhood to have a telephone and a TV, but she was also
known for helping people in need," Edelstein said, who recalls
her mother providing food and clothing to needy families.
Edelstein herself would spend years trying to find her own
niche in the Jewish world. Now a nondenominational rabbi
and an ordained chaplain, she leads services in a New York
nursing home for the elderly.

A Heritage Mislaid

American Jews born in the aftermath of the Holocaust came of
age in the shadow of overwhelming loss and intermittent
harassment. For some, being Jewish seemed more of a liability than a blessing. Certain families changed their names in an
effort to hide their identity and ward off anti-Semitism.
Indeed, Edelstein sensed danger in the mere fact of her religion. In her low-income neighborhood of Brooklyn, with its
cultural stir-fry of Holocaust survivors, Polish and Italian
immigrants, and native-born poor, she learned at a young age

of history's most horrifying Jewish genocide. "I remember the Holocaust survivors referred to as *makis*," recalled Edelstein, who asked her mother, "Why are they calling them that?" Her mother told her four-year-old daughter about the Nazis' crimes against her people. "I associated being Jewish at that time with something frightening," Edelstein said. "The non-Jewish world was something to be feared."

When as a young teen, she plunged into her first book about the Holocaust, she saw that dark period in a different light. Now she was determined to somehow compensate for the tragedy that had befallen her people. "I remember an overwhelming feeling of wanting to make up for the loss of the six million," Edelstein said. She thought, "I have to do something in my lifetime, in their memory." In the intervening decades, a growing acceptance of Jews in schools, workplaces, and politics has made it safe to openly and joyfully explore what it means to be Jewish.

More than a handful of today's seekers grew up with scant knowledge of their Jewish roots. Only a *mezuzah* on the threshold marked as Jewish Rayzl Feuer's childhood home in Brooklyn, New York. Her mother was a Communist, her father an Orthodox Jew who had left his faith behind. "We didn't do Passover; we didn't fast on Yom Kippur," recalled Feuer, now fifty-eight and of Stony Creek, Connecticut. "I didn't know about any of the Jewish holidays." Then, at age nine or ten, she witnessed the blessings over the Chanukah candles at a friend's house: "They said words I'd never heard." In the wake of that experience, her father bought her a tin menorah, candles, and dreidels (tops for spinning). That evening, they stood together at home and lit the Chanukah candles.

"Every night he and I would do this," Feuer said, recalling her father's blessing over the menorah. "I remember the glow of the light. I didn't have the *seichl* (sense) to ask what the words meant: I was like the simple child at the Pesach table."

She remained largely outside the Jewish community until the birth of a child led her to reexamine her religious roots. Teachers in the Jewish Renewal movement helped her put the *seichl* back in Judaism.

Back when Feuer's parents were young, half a century ago and more, many American Jews were striving to assimilate into what was then the majority Christian, Anglo-Saxon culture. Driven by persecution in their countries of origin, discrimination in the United States, and economic pressures or isolation, many changed their names, cut their Jewish ties, and let go of ritual and tradition. Today, with Jews fully integrated into mainstream society, from the business world to the professions and from the arts to politics, some are giving another, searching look at the religious heritage earlier generations set aside or downplayed. But there's a catch to their quest: Jewish institutions set up to serve either the most traditional or the most assimilated often do not meet the needs of Jewish seekers. Such seekers hunger for a sense of meaning, a depth of community, an authentic spirituality that speaks to the eternal challenges of love, work, and family, as well as to such contemporary dilemmas as suburban anomie, environmental destruction, and social inequity.

The drive for spiritual connection, like other human impulses, seeks a channel. Not all of those frustrated by the gap between Jewish ideals and the realities of communal life have been willing to give their faith several chances. As the ensuing stories suggest, many others have hunted for spiritual homes elsewhere.

3 Detours and Switchbacks
Swerving In and Out of Other Faiths

In high school, I haunted the stacks of the public library on Saturdays, browsing my way through the tiny Judaica section in a novice attempt at Shabbat observance. I devoured books on converts, who were not so different in their beginners' wonder and ignorance from my secular self back then. I chewed on the pithy ethical reflections of *Pirke Avot* (literally, "Chapters of the Fathers"), later translated more inclusively by Rabbi Rami Shapiro as Ethics of the Sages (see his book *Ethics of the Sages: Pirke Avot—Annotated & Explained* [SkyLight Paths]).

But my sense of Judaism's riches dissipated as I headed for college. In the cultural stew of the 1970s, Eastern religions were the prized ingredients. It seemed that every other student in my campus co-op was poring over Hinduism's Bhagavad Gita, probing for answers in the Chinese I Ching, or claiming instant adherence to Zen Buddhism. I, too, explored some of these venerable texts and traditions. On the spirituality index of my own boomer generation, the Jewish religion ranked low or simply dropped out of sight. Like many people my age, I overlooked Judaism's resources, discounted its strengths, and dismissed it as a patriarchal system, when, indeed, all of the world's major faiths have much to answer for in their treatment of women.

Reams have been written about how Jews have drifted, sometimes permanently, into Buddhism and other Asian spiritual disciplines. Rodger Kamenetz brilliantly dissected this phenomenon more than a decade ago in his groundbreaking book, *The Jew in the Lotus: A Poet's Rediscovery of Jewish Identity in Buddhist India.* More than a century of assimilation had eroded some of the vital edges of Jewish life. The Holocaust and its aftershocks literally scared some Jews away from their religious moorings. And Jewish wisdom, scattered among a multitude of texts, seemed increasingly out of reach to generations with a minimal grasp of Hebrew. Meanwhile, spirituality dove underground in much of the organized Jewish community. With all this to deal with, some Jews sought the ineffable elsewhere.

Raised a Reform Jew in Grand Rapids, Michigan, singer Randy Herman shelved his religion in college and through his twenties, as he threw himself headlong into one spiritual discipline after another, from Buddhism to Native American sweat lodges and guru-led ashrams. "It literally didn't even occur to me that Judaism would be a place to look," said Herman, now a cantorial student at the Conservative movement's Jewish Theological Seminary in New York.

An encounter with what he called "cool, deep-thinking Orthodox Jews" who could articulate the meaning behind the *mitzvot* (commandments) they followed prompted Herman to give his heritage another glance. Their example led him to stake out the middle ground of Judaism, between the most liberal and traditional poles. In the Halachically rooted but modernity-conscious Conservative movement, Herman found a home. After years as a freewheeling musician, he takes joy in the structure of Jewish observance, from Shabbat to *kashrut* (the kosher laws).

Herman struggles to articulate the difference between his early spiritual experiments and the Jewish life he now pursues. On a day-to-day level, the faith that he reclaimed infuses ordinary life—from speech, to food, to work—with holiness. Put in a larger frame, the religion also links Herman to generations past in a way he finds meaningful. "Judaism as a spiritual pursuit I feel is infinitely more complicated to talk about than Christianity ... and the spiritual paths I used to know," said Herman. "It's subtle, and moment to moment; it has to do with slowly and methodically ... beginning to align oneself with a tribal, communal, ritualistic community that has to do with our personal relationship with an unfolding history." That kind of spiritual alignment intrigues Herman. The Conservative movement, he says, calls him to deeper observance while leaving room for imperfection and growth. "I get to be inconsistent and to struggle with my relationship with Judaism, Jewish practice, and my understanding of what God is," Herman said.

Traveling Other Paths

Deborah Oleshansky might have been another one of those perpetually missing from the minyan, the Jewish quorum of ten needed for crucial prayers. As a Jewish educator working with Tennessee high school and college students, she has plenty of opportunities to counsel young people about the very questions of religious identity that gripped her for years.

Oleshansky harbors warm memories of kindling Shabbat candles next to the red velvet challah cover (the decorative cloth draped over the traditional braided loaf on Sabbath Eve) of her maternal grandmother, a refugee from Nazi Germany. Yet it took her decades and many religious detours to recapture that sense of comfort in Jewish life as an adult. "I always felt a spiritual connection with lighting candles," Oleshansky recalled. "Where I was missing the spiritual connection was in synagogue. I didn't find that until I had traveled other paths and brought it back to my Judaism." After growing up in a large Conservative congregation in suburban Boston, for close to a decade, starting in her early twenties, Oleshansky was a virtual Jewish dropout while she built a career in domestic violence prevention.

It was her move to predominantly Christian Knoxville in 1990 that led her to explore spirituality with ten other women, kindred spirits from her suburban cul-de-sac. "Studying with these women was the water I needed to get through the day," said Oleshansky, one of two Jews in the interreligious group. Discussions with these neighborhood seekers led her to launch a daily Hindu-based meditation practice. From there, she and some of her new friends delved into Native American religious customs, including a medicine wheel, which they used to heal a home built on Indian burial grounds. "In doing the ceremony, I felt God," Oleshansky said. "I felt that strong connection that I had previously only felt in meditation." She had what Jews might call—alluding to the traditional prayer affirming the oneness of God—a *Shema Yisrael* moment, which she described as "really being connected to the oneness of everything."

After sampling spirituality from other traditions, Oleshansky felt ready to approach Judaism again, at first through the Jewish Renewal movement. Today, she belongs to an egalitarian Conservative congregation, Heska Emuna Synagogue, and says her forty-minute daily meditation practice has deepened the religious heritage with which she grew up. "It brought me full circle: it took all of the consciousness work, the quest for universal consciousness, and brought it back into my Judaism," she said. "At my core, I was still Jewish." And the simple act of kindling the Shabbat lights serves as a symbol of her larger purpose in her professional work: "lighting candles" for those around her. In her work with young people, said Oleshansky, that means "helping them understand that their Judaism can be bigger than they can possibly imagine."

A Lingering Ambivalence

For his part, Frank London grew up in the classic Reform movement, which had abandoned many traditional Jewish practices. "We ate our ham and cheese on matzah," London recalled of his boyhood in Plainview, New York. He looks back at his checkered religious upbringing, which did include Hebrew school, with mixed feelings. "It was horrible in that they didn't teach what they had rejected and why," London said of his teachers, but, on the plus side, "there was absolutely no hypocrisy or self-loathing." He emerged with a decided ambivalence about his Jewish roots that lingered from early adolescence until roughly age thirty.

Meanwhile, London sought spiritual nourishment in a smorgasbord of other religions and philosophies, zigzagging from Zen Buddhism to the existentialism of Sartre and Camus, to yoga, to the I Ching and Tibetan Buddhism, from other faiths to euphoria-inducing drugs. "When I felt like I actually had to make a real choice about my belief system ... I couldn't answer the question of why I was born Jewish," London recalled. The search for answers ultimately carried him toward the ebullience of Hasidic Judaism and the hypnotic rhythms of klezmer music. "I think I'm part of a movement—egalitarian, Hasidic, ecstatic," said London. But he stresses that he and his friends part ways with more traditional Hasidic communities on some issues, since "gender separation doesn't work for us and [their] politics is antithetical to our political world, and a xenophobic fear of outsiders is antithetical to a universalistic view."

London typifies those whose early exposure to Judaism was bereft of spiritual depth and relevance. Many people interviewed for this book, who now find themselves at the heart of

Jewish life, did not find the sustenance they needed in their religious upbringing and education. Some have spent years, if not decades, seeking it in other faiths and disciplines. The spiritual wealth of Judaism that enriches the souls of some Jews lies out of reach for others. As we will see in chapter 6, the need for some knowledge of Hebrew to access the tradition poses a daunting barrier for many. Yet those who do find a vehicle for their spirituality outside the Jewish world sometimes find that their path leads them back to their religious beginnings.

As suggested earlier, people who find little meaning in their youthful religious life are at risk of being lost to the Jewish community. Semiretired pharmacist Hershel Sakulsky, of Oceanside, California, had a bar mitzvah that left no spiritual traces. He was the cantor for the day, leading the prayers of the morning service at an Orthodox shul near his home in Rochester, Pennsylvania, a small town outside of Pittsburgh. "I felt something *davening* [fervent praying], but getting up there giving a speech that the rabbi had written didn't do anything for me," said Sakulsky, now sixty-eight. He was touched by the prayers but disengaged from the canned sermon. He found no heartier religious fare at Reform Sunday school, which he recalls as "playtime and history" with no discernible spirituality in the curriculum. Indeed, his boyhood was riven by religious tensions between his Orthodox maternal grandfather and his Reform-affiliated parents, who kept kosher but had become "atheists to agnostics" in their attitude toward Judaism.

Once on his own in college, Sakulsky quit his religion and went on to marry a Presbyterian woman who soon joined the Jehovah's Witnesses. Their union was stormy, and Sakulsky took a drastic step to save it. "Long story made short, I converted to try to help my marriage," said Sakulsky, who spent thirty-five "roller-coaster" years as a Jehovah's Witness. Yet through decades in his adoptive faith, he never quite abandoned his Jewish roots. "When I would study and read about

King David and Absalom and all the patriarchs, I would feel a kinship," Sakulsky said. "They were my people."

When Sakulsky quit the Jewish community, he entered a highly ordered faith with distinct traditions of its own. At first, he liked the overlap with Judaism in the Witnesses' belief in the humanity—rather than the divinity—of Jesus and in its "messianic hopes." These echoed the Jewish dreams of a messiah he'd heard from a pious grandfather. Sakulsky became an elder in his new religion, shepherding other families in their studies, sometimes teaching the entire congregation, even guest lecturing on prescribed topics at other Jehovah's Witnesses' churches. His public face belonged to his new religion, but inner conflict dogged him through three and a half decades away from Judaism. "Down deep inside, I still felt a kinship with the Jewish people, a Jewish soul," Sakulsky said.

Meanwhile, he stuck with the "ups and downs" of a turbulent marriage, partly for the sake of his two daughters and three grandchildren. "I wanted to be an example to them," he said. Then, one day, something shifted for him. To be true to himself, he realized, he had to leave both his marriage and his faith. "I felt I was an actor on a stage," Sakulsky said, "playing a role with a mask on."

After his divorce, a counselor suggested a Jewish online dating service as a way to rebuild his shattered community. He tried it and met women who lent him Jewish books, as he sought to rediscover the world he'd left behind. A memoir by Kirk Douglas, *Climbing the Mountain: My Search for Meaning*, particularly stirred him. Sakulsky shares the actor's regrets about how his distance from Judaism had robbed his children of their heritage. The *V'havta* prayer, which calls for teaching Jewish values to one's offspring, "gives me a pang of guilt," Sakulsky said. But he now enjoys Friday night services with his recent bride, Jessica, who turned out to be a member of the Reform congregation in which he first set foot after years away from Judaism. "I'm home where I belong," said Sakulsky, who had his first Jewish wedding last spring. "It's just one blessing after another, and I was supposed to be a cursed person, according to the Jehovah's Witnesses."

Excommunicated from his former faith, Sakulsky has paid a stiff price. He is shunned by many who were once close to him, including his daughters and grandchildren. Yet he credits the Jehovah's Witnesses with the pivotal role it played in his spiritual odyssey. "It awakened a spiritual side of me that I never knew existed," which the Witnesses did not fulfill, Sakulsky said. "There was something still lacking, and Judaism has filled that."

Detours That Lead Homeward

Like Sakulsky, some Jews who sample other faiths report that these side trips open doors to a spirituality they later will explore in Judaism. Connie Songer, the Pennsylvania nurse who didn't learn of her Jewish parentage until her mid-thirties, found a bridge between her Methodist rearing and the Jewish world in the Religious Society of Friends. "I really credit Quaker meeting for bringing me to Judaism in a spiritual sense," Songer said. In this silent worship, she could "sit and focus and connect with God in a way that allowed me to get beyond the dogmas that had constrained me in Christianity." That comfortable encounter with the Divine later led her to delve into Jewish practice with less trepidation than she might have felt in a single leap from one tradition to the next. "It opened the door," said Songer of her Quaker experience.

Margot Barnet, a chiropractor, tells a similar story, with the Society of Friends serving as a way station on her journey back to Judaism. Born Jewish and raised Unitarian for much of her childhood, Barnet calls the Quaker meetings she attended "foundational" in her spiritual evolution. "Here was a group of people who took being part of this inner exploration seriously," said Barnet, fifty-four. But her contact with Quaker women who were studying the Christian underpinnings of their faith catapulted Barnet into reappraising her own religious origins. "I felt like I hit a wall," said Barnet. "And I said, 'I can't do this, this is not who I am, this is not where I'm going' and that is what impelled me to do a one hundred-eighty-degree turn and find out where my own roots are."

She began by taking a reading tour of Jewish teachings, even while she was living in a West Virginia commune with its own free-form religious services that were unmoored to any particular faith tradition. "I remember sitting in a tepee and reading books on Judaism," said Barnet, now a member of a Reform congregation in Worcester, Massachusetts.

Just as many people try out several careers before gravitating to one (or more) that fits their skills and talents, seekers often experiment with a range of spiritual pursuits as they discern what speaks to their souls. In her twenties, Stephanie Ozer was drawn toward a female-centered spirituality and spent some years exploring goddess worship while living in Ann Arbor, Michigan. "I left the Bronx and East Coast Jews behind during that phase of my life, and the discovering of previous matriarchal societies was a reassurance during the political and social confusion of the early seventies," Ozer replied when asked about the appeal of this belief system. She enjoyed seeing "women being audacious, strong, knowing (and in power) ... taking care of their bodies from a feminine point of view."

Ozer, a jazz pianist, sought insight from Tarot readings, goddess circles, and sweat lodge ceremonies, but never made the ultimate commitment of joining a coven. "I always felt so Jewish, and couldn't renounce it for another religion," Ozer wrote, when asked why she didn't pursue this path. "I started to see the wounds so many women (myself included) were attempting to heal, and that anger and judgment was a large part of those groups, too. It didn't quite feel like 'home,' though

I love the perspectives and balance I learned there." In time, she joined a Reform congregation in California's Sonoma County, where she resettled with her husband, David. They wanted to give their son, Gabriel, a Jewish sense of self in their rural corner of the West Coast.

The idea of a "spiritual fit" often comes up among those who have embarked on Jewish journeys. David Blumenstein looks back on his ventures down other spiritual paths as akin to trying on footwear, one at a time. "That shoe was beautiful, but it doesn't fit me," said the Virginia man of his experiments in faith. After studying philosophy in college, exploring Buddhism, and getting involved in human potential movements, he found his way back into Jewish life through books. After reading twentieth-century theologian Abraham Joshua Heschel's *The Sabbath*, Blumenstein saw the Jewish day of rest in a new light: "All of a sudden, the Sabbath was alive for me." He came to believe that a daily religious routine "allows you to understand things in a way that just thinking about it does not"—much as physical workouts build strength over time. "While reading Locke, Kant, and Husserl, I was missing a spiritual practice," he explained.

Blumenstein ultimately found what he sought in Judaism, but credits his detours into other spiritual disciplines with teaching him important lessons along the way. In books by Heschel and rabbi and prolific author Lawrence Kushner, he discovered Jewish perspectives that spoke to his deepest yearnings. But he carried the meditation he had learned elsewhere back into Judaism. "I owe a great debt to the spirit traditions I've gotten to study," Blumenstein said, calling them "catalysts for my Jewish path."

Wisdom from Two Wells

Detours and even continuing side trips into some spiritual byways do not necessarily detract from Jewish commitment.

Certain disciplines, such as meditation, yoga, and martial arts, can actually deepen the *kavanah* (focus) of prayer and traditional ritual, practitioners say. Some have developed personal routines in which these other methods serve as a warm-up for Jewish practice.

While studying for her adult bat mitzvah, Debra Kolodny, forty-seven, of Silver Spring, Maryland, also began her practice of tai chi. Her studies of East and West have chugged along on parallel tracks. The ancient Chinese martial art complements, rather than competes with, her Judaism, says Kolodny, the executive director of ALEPH: Alliance for Jewish Renewal. "I learned a lot of Torah from the Tao," said Kolodny, the editor of *Blessed Bi Spirit: Bisexual People of Faith*. "I came to associate chi [life force] with the God-field."

The dance-like moves of tai chi are now part of her morning routine. She does one short martial arts sequence, sits in meditation for half an hour, then spends twenty-five minutes in Jewish prayer. Citing injunctions by Talmudic sages to meditate before prayer, Kolodny sees this practice as integral to Judaism. "I bring the altered, elevated consciousness I cultivate in the tai chi and the sitting into the *davening* to make it higher, and to make *devekut* [cleaving] to God more likely and more potent," Kolodny said about her routine. Even as she is apprenticing to teach tai chi, Kolodny is also studying for the rabbinate in the Jewish Renewal movement.

Kolodny's spiritual evolution points up the way in which choice often trumps tradition in the creation of contemporary Jewish lives. Back in the Old World days of arranged marriages (which persist in the most traditional corners of the Jewish world), couples usually stayed together for a lifetime, in relationships that likely ranged from the passionate to the poisonous. People generally did not have a full voice in choosing their mates. Religious life followed much the same trajectory. Those born Jewish largely remained so, except when forced conversions or the desire for professional mobility pushed some out of the community. The welcome fall of ghettoes and the decline, for a time, of persecution brought Jews into the mainstream of Western societies, where they had both more freedom and weaker ties to their home communities. As anti-Semitic discrimination in the United States abated over the second half of the twentieth century, Jews gained access to work in a full range of professions and homes in any neighborhood they could afford. As barriers fell, being Jewish became more of a choice than an inevitability, as commentators such as Rabbi Sidney Schwarz, author of *Finding a Spiritual Home* (Jewish Lights), and Stuart M. Matlins, founder of Jewish Lights Publishing, have noted.

Yet some synagogues have continued to operate as if they had no spiritual competition. As suggested in this chapter, many people, young and old, who grew up in the heart of the Jewish community came of age seemingly untouched by religious relevance. Some members of the baby boom generation, with its slogan, "Question authority," were unwilling to blindly follow the faith of their forebears. For good or for ill, the values of the marketplace also have influenced Jewish commitment, as people go "shul shopping" or appraise the features of spiritual options outside Judaism.

For some wandering Jews, exploring other traditions is a detour, one that ultimately leads, after more than a few twists and turns, back to a more fruitful Jewish experience. As their stories unfold, it seems that any encounter along the road—be it the people they meet, the communities in which they walk, the media they see and read—has the potential to redirect their steps. Yet the seeming randomness of their spiritual switchbacks hints at the unknowable number of Jews who may remain lost to their heritage along the way, never finding a sign, a guide, or a trail trodden by others to lead them homeward. It is partly with them in mind that I wrote this book.

4 Dipping a Toe in the *Mikvah*
First Steps to a Jewish Life

E than Seidel climbed a musical path back into Jewish life. Returning from a youthful detour into Quaker meetings, he vowed to master one of Judaism's most challenging ritual skills: trope, the traditional chanting of the Torah. "Music has always had this ability to speak to me and say things you can't say any other way," said Seidel, fifty, now a rabbi in Washington, D.C.

For this student of piano, the haunting strains of Hebrew trope offered a key to the palace of spiritual connection. "When you're singing something that old to words that old, it's a very powerful thing," said Seidel, who learned trope from a fellow student at Oberlin College. "You're linked to a musical tradition that's very ancient." As he made these sacred melodies his own, Seidel—once a rebel railing against religious hypocrisy—embarked on a voyage that would challenge him to switch careers and take him deeper into Jewish life than he ever imagined.

As Seidel intuitively knew, to fully inhabit a Jewish identity means to do—to learn; to participate in Judaism's fabric of celebration, prayer, and ritual; and to try to behave in the home, the community, and the larger world with kindness and justice in mind. To be a Jew is not so much to believe, a key to their faith for many Christians, as to act in the private and public spheres in accordance with Jewish values and Jewish law.

Jews may ground their faith in deeds, but they follow different paths of action, depending on their religious leanings. Orthodox Jews strive to follow the bulk of 613 *mitzvot* set forth in the Torah; liberal Jews tend to choose their *mitzvot* with an eye to balancing tradition and modernity. Wherever they fall on the spectrum of observance and belief, many Jewish seekers report powerful reverberations from their first steps toward reclaiming their religious heritage.

Leila Gal Berner's early moves in that direction took her into a Los Angeles gay and lesbian synagogue and the first Jewish services she had ever witnessed. At work on a doctorate in medieval history, Berner was simply seeking to meet some other Jews. She found far more than new friends. Fresh from a decade in Israel, where she was not religiously involved, the Hebrew-literate Berner grasped the meaning of the prayers at Beth Chayim Chadashim. She liked what she heard. "I fell in love with the liturgy—it was profound, aesthetic, poetic, and the images were gorgeous," said Berner. As she became a regular at the congregation, its leaders quickly noticed her mastery of Hebrew and tapped her to chair the liturgy committee. "I said yes and started one of the steepest learning curves ever," said Berner, who ended up leading many services at the synagogue. The joy she discovered in this role took her by surprise.

"Opening up that prayer book, I realized there was a whole world of spiritual and religious Judaism that I didn't know," said Berner, now fifty-seven and a Reconstructionist rabbi living in Kensington, Maryland. "Once I started exploring, I was like a kid in a candy shop—I couldn't stop."

Kindling Lights in a New Place

Isolation from a large, thriving Jewish community can erode the edges of Jewish identity—or it can build them up. Surrounded by other faiths and cultures, some lose their own ethnic and religious moorings. Others rediscover them. When Hershel Weiss left New York for New Mexico two decades ago, the move threw his Jewish identity into relief as sharp as the desert landscape around his new home in Albuquerque. "Suddenly, it became really important that I was a Jew because there were so few of us," Weiss said. Moved by the spirituality of a local rabbi, Lynn Gottlieb, Weiss began attending services at Gottlieb's Jewish Renewal congregation. "I saw the humanity, the intelligence, the importance of justice and care for the world in the ceremonies themselves and in her interpretations of the liturgy," said Weiss, fifty-five.

Raised by Communist parents in the Bronx, New York, Weiss harbored memories of his Orthodox grandparents fasting, with difficulty, on Yom Kippur and praying at a neighborhood shul (synagogue). "I'd be asked to bring smelling salts up to the women's balcony for my grandmother, and then my father would take me out for pizza," Weiss said of the family traditions dueling for his loyalty. Yet Weiss retained a strong sense of the sacred from his grandparents' religious life. "In the Orthodox shul, I got to experience what prayer really was," said Weiss. With old men all around him "praying hard," he recalled, "I could really feel something was going on."

Taking his first steps toward an adult Jewish life in his mid-thirties, Weiss began lighting candles on Friday night. That ritual transformed his life. Soon, he had stopped driving on the Sabbath, as part of an effort to slow down and avoid use of human technology. As a result, said Weiss, "I am able to taste something different" on this day of rest. After two decades of experimentation, he calls his Shabbat observance "still a work in progress."

Facing Mortality, Finding Spirituality

David Abraham gave Judaism a second chance after two dramatic life passages—a neighbor's violent death and his son's bar mitzvah, which took place a month after the September 11 terrorist attacks on New York's World Trade Center and the Pentagon. These reminders of mortality surfaced around the time the Miami lawyer, forty-seven, was fielding religious questions from an old friend. Their conversations left Abraham feeling abashed about his paper-thin knowledge of his own heritage.

Visiting his family's Conservative synagogue, which he had largely avoided up until then, Abraham "sat as far away from other people as I could because I was embarrassed about how little Hebrew I knew and how little I remembered of what a Saturday morning service is about." That first step led to others. Abraham found that he enjoyed meeting other congregants and learning with them. "It was easy to pull meaning from the sermons," he said of his congregation's rabbi, Ed Farber. Inspired by another local rabbi, Rabbi Efrat Zarren Zohar, Abraham committed to a year's study in the Florence Melton Adult Mini-School. "Judaism is basically this treasure chest and I just had never opened it," Abraham said of his religious rediscovery. "The amazing thing is that I didn't realize I had the key." Now a vice president of the synagogue, he wants to make it more welcoming to Jews on the margins of their community, where he once stood.

Out on the West Coast, Terry Spodick once paid her dues to her local Reform temple "so it would be there for others, so the Jewish heritage would continue." A proverbial two-day-a-year Jew who breezed in on the Jewish High Holy Days, Rosh Hashanah and Yom Kippur, the Santa Cruz resident spent most of her time marketing the Jewish greeting cards she designs and helping nurture the area's small businesses.

That all changed when a terminal lymphoma diagnosis sixteen years ago catapulted her into a spiritual journey. As she cultivated her inner life with a new urgency, she and her husband began lighting candles on Friday night and counting the week's blessings. "We're grateful if we get through a week without a major trauma," said Spodick, who, despite the original diagnosis, is fully recovered but now has several elderly relatives in various states of ill health. Raised Jewish by interfaith parents, she had resisted efforts at conversion during seven years in a Catholic boarding school, where she landed after her parents' divorce. Yet it took cancer for her to give Jewish spirituality another serious look. "I've always felt Judaism was my heritage," said Spodick. "I think what's in your heart and the way you act on it is ultimately the most important thing."

Exploring Paths of Ritual

Once a secular Jew, Stephen Landau began his road to rabbinical school with a set of *tefillin*. These are the small leather boxes attached to leather straps and containing biblical verses, which traditional Jewish men and some women wear over the arm and forehead during weekday morning prayers. Landau, fifty-three, had already sampled careers in carpentry, contracting, massage therapy, and community outreach. Raised on "Yiddish and matzah balls" in Dallas, Texas, he spent close to two decades exploring non-Jewish spiritual disciplines. For more than fifteen years, he was involved in the Transcendental Meditation movement, and in the early 1980s he spent summers in the ecumenical Lama Foundation, an intentional community in New Mexico.

During a 1985 workshop at Lama with Jewish Renewal leader Rabbi Zalman M. Schachter-Shalomi, author of *First Steps to a New Jewish Spirit* (Jewish Lights), Landau donned his first *tefillin* and promptly burst into tears. "I had this visceral experience I was not prepared for," said Landau, who reports "imagining all of my male ancestors, starting with my grandfather" performing the same ritual. The last step of donning *tefillin*—which involves winding a leather strap around the middle finger and saying verses from Hosea: "I will betroth you to me forever; I will betroth you to me in righteousness, justice, kindness, and mercy; I will betroth you to me in faithfulness; and you will know God"—particularly struck a chord for him. "During all those years of spiritual seeking, I wanted to know God and have a relationship with God," explained Landau, a student at the Rabbinical School of Hebrew College in Newton Centre, Massachusetts. "When I put them [*tefillin*] on, I am reaffirming that I am committing to God."

The notion of prayer was as foreign as Hebrew to Natasha Hirschhorn when the Ukrainian-born New Yorker launched her own Jewish journey. Soviet repression had shadowed her family—one grandfather, a theater critic, was executed on spying charges; a set of great-grandparents, active in Yiddish theater, died in prison camps; and a grandmother raised Hirschhorn's mother in a Siberian concentration camp. "There's all this darkness, a black hole you can feel," recalled Hirschhorn, a thirty-six-year-old who grew up with "a sense of Jewishness as a liability."

In her first attempts at reclaiming Judaism, she began adopting rituals as simple as the blessing before meals. "Prayer was a far-out concept I [now] can't imagine being without," said Hirschhorn, who sees the opening phrase—*Baruch Atah Ha-Shem Eloheynu Melech ha-olam* ("Blessed are you, Lord, Sovereign of the universe")—as a set of "ever widening circles" that transport you from communion with the Divine to a link with infinity. "In six words, you travel from an intimate connection to the Creator to connection with all of the universe," said Hirschhorn. "You recall that God is all of the world."

In his own experiments with Jewish practice, academic Richard Chused started small. "The image of Jacob's ladder is a real one for us—one step at a time," said Chused of his religious evolution. He and his wife, Elizabeth, he says, began kindling the Sabbath candles, adding prayers to their Friday evening ritual, inviting guests to their table, and roasting a chicken for the occasion.

Their first encounter with a full Shabbat came two decades ago on a "transformative" family retreat for bar and bat mitzvah families at their Conservative synagogue. For twenty-five hours, he and his wife—two high-powered Washingtonians—lived without a telephone, television, or computer. Reading, conversation, and prayer filled the hours usually cluttered with electronic communication. Today, Chused relishes their weekly Shabbat observance: "It puts the rest of your life in perspective, it puts you into a different rhythm, and it's very relaxing."

Following Hearts and Talents

Composer, painter, and psychologist Norma Brooks exploited her artistic talents to forge an adult relationship with Judaism. Shortly after joining a Boston *chavurah* some thirty years ago, this New York native honored a congregant's bat mitzvah by pulling out her paintbrushes. She produced a watercolor of a woman wrapped in a *tallit* flanked by trees reaching skyward and surrounded by the Hebrew inscriptions *"Havu Godel l'Elohenu ut'nu khavod la'Torah"* ("Ascribe greatness to our God and give honor to the Torah") from the Torah service and *"Etz chayim hi lamachazikim bah v'tomkheha me'ushar"* ("It is a tree of life to those who hold it fast, and all who support it are made happy"). "For me, the first steps are connected to: What can I create?" said Brooks, now sixty and of Chevy Chase, Maryland. "I was very drawn to people doing *ketubot* [marriage contracts] and illuminations." This began decades of crafting artwork and, later, liturgical compositions, in honor of passages such as births, deaths, and anniversaries in her circle of friends and family. As Brooks put illustrations and melodies to Hebrew texts, the ancient words took on life for her.

It may seem premature to touch on a fifteen-year-old's Jewish journey, yet a Massachusetts rabbi referred me to a teen congregant whose passion for Judaism has already transformed her life. Hanna Switlekowski, of Sharon, Massachusetts, grew up largely secular, but her involvement with a social action project at her Reform congregation drew her into religious practice. Switlekowski was one of the first young people to take part in the project—a monthly dinner for the men of a Boston homeless shelter; soon she was enlisting other peers to join in. "It's definitely made me want to do more for my community," Switlekowski said. "When I started, I didn't know there were so many homeless."

In 2006, the temple helped support her trip to the Ukraine and Israel, an experience that deepened her "religious Reform" identity. In both places, she spent time in congregations that were more traditional than her own. "Sometimes I think of myself as everything," said Switlekowski of her denominational leanings, "because I wear my *kippah* and *tallit* every Shabbat and the Orthodox [women] can't, but being exposed to the Orthodox, I do some things that are Orthodoxy." This includes adopting the modest dress favored by Orthodox women when she goes to synagogue.

Yet her ambitions remain in the realm of liberal Judaism, as she looks toward possible careers as a Jewish professional. "I definitely see myself doing something with my Judaism," said Switlekowski, who already helps lead services for her congregation. She is considering a future as a rabbi, cantor, or Jewish educator. Wherever her interests lead her, the road ahead is liable to loop and meander toward a Jewish destination, as it has for those who have been journeying for much longer than Switlekowski.

Meanwhile, the man who tutored Ethan Seidel in Hebrew trope left the college they were both attending and turned up years later as a guest at a Lincoln, Nebraska, synagogue then led by his former pupil. In the interim, the ancient melodies of Torah had taken Seidel deeper into Jewish practice. After studying math and music in college and a stint as a computer programmer, he immersed himself in the religion he'd grown up with and once rejected. Now a rabbi for some two decades, he bicycles to work at Tifereth Israel Congregation, a Conservative synagogue in Washington, D.C. "I wasn't looking to dip my toes in," Seidel said of the heritage he reclaimed. "I couldn't wait to take the full *mikvah* [ritual bath], the full bath."

Ethan Seidel pursued his passion for music into the melodies of Jewish prayer. Leila Gal Berner turned her Hebrew skills to leading services. These choices opened religious and professional paths for both seekers. These two lives manifest, even in their differences, a piece of common ground. On the spiritual journey, each step brings its own momentum. If there are lessons to be learned from the disparate tales in this chapter, these stories of spiritual beginnings, they are: Start somewhere. Follow your heart and talents. Horizons will open.

For most of us on the Jewish journey, taking the first steps homeward requires courage and the will to overcome inertia and old habits, even congenial ones. Cooking a special meal and reciting a blessing over candles, wine and challah on Erev Shabbat, instead of heading for happy hour drinks with co-workers, for instance, calls for a willingness to resist impulse, even peer pressure, and a determination to readjust the rhythms of our lives to a deeper music than mere routine. I have always loved the down-to-earth advice of the Rabbinic Sages on the challenge of learning and living Torah (*Pirke Avot* 2:21): "You are not expected to complete the task. Nor are you free to set it aside." The key is to begin.

5 Scouts in the Wilderness
Mentors Point the Way

Jewish values take on their deepest meaning in the daily lives of ordinary people. All seekers blaze their own trails, but the words and deeds of those farther along a spiritual path are promises of a journey worth taking. Faith with a face—be it that of a grandparent, a teacher, or a stranger met in passing— makes the tenets of religion real.

The Jewish world can seem like a maze to the outsider. Jews who have grown up without religious schooling or the embrace of a Jewish community often have trouble finding a way in. To them, the landscape of Judaism seems studded with twists, turns, and secret byways that only the initiated can navigate. No wonder that mentors figure prominently in the stories of so many returning Jews. The people who can help "translate" the folkways of Jewish life—the "*yasher koach*" said in congratulation to someone who has just played a ritual, ceremonial, or educational role in the Jewish community; the new beard grown after the death of a parent—as well as the larger meaning of religious practices, ease the road home to Judaism.

The Torah relates that after forty years of wandering in the wilderness, Moses sent a dozen men out to scout Canaan, the Promised Land (Numbers 13). The advance team came back with fruits of the season—grapes, figs, and pomegranates—but mixed reports of Canaan. Most of the scouts stressed the dangers in the territory ahead, telling of a fearsome place that "devours its inhabitants" (Num. 13:22). Only Joshua and Caleb appreciated the area's potential, depicting a "land that flows with milk and honey" (Num. 14:8).

For the Jewish seeker, this story hints at the role played by those who walk ahead of us on the spiritual journey. They can preview the terrain to come—its pitfalls and possibilities—and offer ideas on how to venture forward. Yet, the biblical scouts, with their wildly varying reports, suggest another lesson: it makes sense to take all religious advice with a grain of kosher salt! In the end, our journey is our own.

Today, in the American Diaspora, Jewish "scouts" or mentors play a variety of roles. Some field questions—practical ones, like what to bring to the seder, and existential ones, like what Judaism has to say about evil. Other mentors provide spiritual companionship, in the tradition of the *chevruta* (study partner). And some mentors simply model the lovingkindness, integrity, and moral courage that draws those they touch into Jewish practice.

A Brush with Greatness

For photographer Lloyd Wolf, a chance encounter during his college years with the late Jewish theologian Rabbi Abraham Joshua Heschel—the author of *The Sabbath* and other books on Judaism, a professor of Jewish ethics and mysticism at The Jewish Theological Seminary, a civil rights activist, and a theological giant of the twentieth century—threw a fresh light on

Judaism. Wolf, now of Arlington, Virginia, sports a ponytail and an affable manner that can mask his intellectual curiosity. In the fall of 1972, he was working on the campus newspaper at Trinity College in Hartford, Connecticut. One Sunday, the twenty-year-old photo editor was readying pictures and captions for the next day's edition. Heschel's daughter, Susannah, later a pioneer of Jewish feminism, then edited the paper, and her short, white-bearded father dropped by her office.

A keen observer of people, Wolf recalls watching, "transfixed," as the famous rabbi walked down the narrow, faux-medieval hallway. What struck the young photographer was the quiet power of Heschel's bearing. "I felt I was in the presence of someone in the direct living tradition of Moses, Aaron, Hillel, and Maimonides—and it looked good," Wolf said. Wolf suddenly sensed a better way to elevate his soul than through the psychedelic drugs he had experimented with. "At that point, I began my Jewish tradition," he said. "I was sober but I experienced him glowing." By the end of the year, the elder Heschel was dead and Wolf was delving into the celebrated rabbi's writings.

Today, the photographer credits his brush with Heschel as a turning point on the road toward Jewish engagement. Raised with minimal Jewish practice at home, Wolf shifted from reading about Eastern religions to exploring Jewish mysticism. "I'd been trying on every hat but Judaism," he said. Poring over the densely worded pages of Heschel's *God in Search of Man* and *The Prophets: An Introduction*, he gleaned two crucial lessons. "God, being infinite, appears at all places and all times," explained Wolf, so people in different faith traditions can access the Divine. Yet, "for Jews, for me, Judaism is the right way to approach God," he concluded. Once started, Wolf continued walking a Jewish road.

Where Family Leaves Off

For many, remaining on that road while growing up in a majority Christian environment takes a strong inner compass.

It can be hard to navigate the currents of peer pressure and the sometimes more subtle blandishments of schools and communities, which often schedule important tests on Jewish holidays or sports events on Shabbat.

Mentors can also help young people with parents who are ambivalent about Judaism. Raised in an assimilated Atlanta family, Myriam Klotz found a religious guide in a time of adolescent angst. As a Jewish teen, she was sent to a Christian school for its strong academic program. While there, Klotz struggled with questions of faith raised by reading such authors as theologian Dietrich Bonhoeffer and novelist C. S. Lewis. As her spiritual self awakened, she found herself drawn to the personal God of Christianity. To give Klotz another perspective, her mother put her in touch with professor David Blumenthal, a Jew who then chaired the Religion Department at Emory University. He offered to meet with Klotz on Shabbat afternoons to discuss her concerns. Sitting with him, sometimes for hours at a stretch, Klotz was struck by his generosity. He apologized once for not being available on Rosh Hashanah. On that day, it was his custom to go with his son to the nursing home to blow the shofar for the residents.

"What he embodied was as important as what he spoke," said Klotz, now a Reconstructionist rabbi who directs the yoga and embodied practices at the Institute for Jewish Spirituality in New York and is a spiritual director, or counselor, at the Reconstructionist Rabbinical College. Blumenthal, a scholar of Jewish theology, mysticism, and medieval and Holocaust history, became, for the questioning teen, "my first rabbi in every sense of the word—pastor, mentor, presence." Said Klotz, "He started to give me a sense that there was a possibility for a deeply reflective, contemplative spiritual life in Judaism."

Mentors do not have to be older than the people they inspire. In fact, peers on their own spiritual journey make

wonderful traveling companions, as Jonathan Rosenfield discovered. Rosenfield's boyhood home in Nyack, New York, was
a spiritual mishmash: Christmas gifts sat across the room
from the Chanukah menorah. His secular parents sent him to
a Sunday school that taught Jewish culture, but not religion.
He gleaned a bit of Yiddish and Holocaust history from his
classes, but no Hebrew or larger sense of Jewish values. "I
didn't like it," Rosenfield said. "It didn't resonate for me spiritually or intellectually."

Then in seventh grade, he met a kindred spirit with religious leanings. Brian Schachter-Brooks, the son of a Catholic
mother and a Jewish father, was enthralled with the Zohar,
the cornerstone sacred text of the Jewish mystical tradition.
Rosenfield caught the fever. "In some way, I was swept along
on his journey," said Rosenfield, who remembers their
"intense intellectual discussions about God, the nature of the
universe." Jewish teachings were richer than he had known,
Rosenfield said: Brian "showed me that the stuff I'd been
exposed to in Sunday school was not the be-all and end-all of
Judaism." His friendship with Brian was a spiritual "place-
holder," Rosenfield said, that kept him loosely tied to his religious roots until he would reclaim them in adulthood. Indeed,
it was Brian who would help his buddy find a niche in the
Jewish Renewal movement when Rosenfield settled in
Northern California decades later. "When I was ready to
explore that germ of an interest, Brian was there as a
resource," said Rosenfield, who now belongs to Chochmat
HaLev, a Berkeley congregation.

Rabbis of the Soul

People from families that keep Judaism at arm's length often
are eager to meet the kind of "embodied" Jew Myriam Klotz
and Rosenfield found in their own mentors. As we have seen,
those encounters can redirect lives. Take SaraHope Smith, a

magenta-haired punk rocker turned biodiesel cooperative worker and environmental studies graduate student. Her spiritual course shifted after a single radio public service announcement.

For years, Smith labeled herself "not religious but spiritual." Apart from attending a seder and lighting Chanukah candles, she did nothing Jewish. The Berkeley, California, woman, now forty, changed her mantra one day in the mid-1990s. While crunching data for a financial services firm, Smith switched on a progressive radio station. The voice of Rabbi Michael Lerner came on, talking about upcoming High Holy Day services he would be conducting in the area. Something in Lerner's eclectic approach conjured up "a place where all of me can be accepted—the intellectual, the spiritual, the social." Attending services at Beyt Tikkun, the Berkeley congregation led by this rabbi and social justice activist, Smith found herself "wowed" by his message: "the God you don't believe in doesn't exist—you're here to worship what you do believe in."

Like Rosenfield, Smith came from a religiously mixed family, with a Jewish mother and a Lutheran father. She had a spotty Reform education, though she credits her mother for trying to suffuse Jewish practice with meaning. These days, Smith calls herself "flexidoxic" or "neo-Hasidic." Thanks to mentors like Lerner, she is piecing together the disparate bits of her growing Jewish knowledge. "Now, the way I understand Judaism, there's so much fabric that connects the pieces," said Smith, who still calls Michael Lerner "the rabbi of my soul," although she has been part of various Jewish communities.

A member of a Conservative synagogue, David Blumenstein has developed eclectic tastes in his Judaism—and spiritual mentors. These include such Jewish Renewal teachers as Rabbi Shefa Gold and Blumenstein's own rabbi at Agudas Achim Congregation in Alexandria, Virginia, Rabbi

Jack Moline. As a community activist and dynamic speaker, Moline models "being in the world and not flinching from it." Added Blumenstein, "That's what I aspire to."

Joanne Doades encountered another powerful rabbinic figure when she ventured into New York's Central Synagogue in the early 1980s. There the New Jersey woman met Rabbi Sheldon Zimmerman, who kindled an abiding interest in Jewish life for Doades and a host of others. "He held an incredible ability to take the Torah—no matter how arcane—and translate it into the present moment, so you could resolve a problem in your own life," Doades said. She was among a circle of students who clustered around him in the mid- to late-1980s, several of whom now work in the Jewish world. "People went on to take their Judaism very seriously," said Doades. She later walked away from a career in the corporate world, as a marketing representative for IBM, to raise her children and become a Jewish educator for the Reform movement.

A lifetime as a secular Jew can leave a person out of the habit of spiritual self-discovery. Sometimes it takes a mentor to convey the message: Go ahead. Plunge in. The water's warm. After his dispiriting brush with a boyhood rabbi and decades in the Communist Party, Melvin Metelits kept his distance from Judaism. When he began reappraising his religious roots, he kept his change of heart a secret from his old associates. "I was embarrassed to let my old comrades, many of whom were still my friends, know what I was considering," Metelits said.

The day he attended a Jewish service for the first time in close to fifty years, he met Rabbi Zalman M. Schachter-Shalomi as he was entering the synagogue and told him of the milestone. The rabbi stopped to offer a blessing, which Metelits later remembered as a Jewish prayer said after hearing good news. Later, as the newcomer sat alone in the back of the Philadelphia congregation, he became aware of a presence next to him. "Suddenly I felt a gentle tap on my shoulder and there he was with the *tallit* to put on," said Metelits. This gesture of inclusion by a man he now calls his mentor felt like the "ultimate welcoming."

The service that followed hit home as the former Marxist sat draped in the prayer shawl. "When the morning prayer began, my heart burst open because I heard singing and *davening* with such energy that I had never experienced in any synagogue," Metelits said. The passionate worship shocked him out of his spiritual detachment. He realized there was something he had been lacking, even in a life enriched by political activism and his work as an elementary schoolteacher. "When my heart opened, I knew I had experienced what I couldn't grasp with my intellect," explained Metelits, adding that "with all the good I did, this was a missing dimension in my life—the opening of the heart." He would go on to become a *maggid*, or trained storyteller, in the Jewish Renewal movement.

Guides in Unusual Garb

Some seekers have found kindred spirits in Jewish personalities from the past. These figures from sacred text, communal history, and family lore can still influence the spiritual quests of contemporary Jews. When nurse Connie Songer discovered at midlife that she was Jewish, congregants at her Pennsylvania synagogue, Temple Beth Shalom of Greater Harrisburg, helped her acclimate to Judaism. Friends there would tell her, "'This is what my mother did, what my grandmother did,'" Songer said. At a crucial time in her life, true stories from the extended families of others gave her a sense of how to celebrate Shabbat and the Jewish holidays in her own home.

Reconstructionist Rabbi Hava Pell has also traveled back in time to draw spiritual insight from one of her own ancestors, the famous eighteenth-century Lithuanian rabbi, Eliyahu of Vilna. Also known as the Vilna Gaon, or "genius," he has appeared in her dreams since her girlhood. In adulthood, Pell lacquered her living room "Vilna red" without knowing its name. "I can't imagine that in his day [the Gaon] would have supported women rabbis, but he's always been there for me," said Pell. "When I get scared spiritually, he's the one who tells me to put one foot in front of the other and continue on this path." The Gaon favored judgment over compassion in religious matters. Seeking to avoid his mistake, or its opposite, Pell aims to keep those two traits in balance on her own spiritual journey.

For Pell, mentors have arrived in all kinds of guises, some from outside the Jewish community. In her daily prayer and meditation, she tries to listen for guidance, whatever its source. "It doesn't matter if it's Thich Nhat Hanh, St. Ignatius, Bill W. and Dr. Bob, one of my Reconstructionist colleagues, or some Hasidic singing group that I love," Pell said, citing a Vietnamese Buddhist activist-monk, the Catholic founder of the Jesuit order, and the founders of Alcoholics Anonymous, among others. From all of these, she says she has learned to acknowledge mistakes, make amends, and move on. "There is truth with a capital *T*, and it is loving compassion, acceptance of our humanness, and the knowledge that God created us as humans and expects us to have human reactions," said Pell, explaining the lessons she has learned from a variety of spiritual figures.

Pell, who left work as a congregational rabbi some years ago to help others with their spiritual journeys, pays tribute to her students, calling them "my greatest teachers." She mentions, for example, a woman in one of the spirituality groups she leads who has survived a diagnosis of stage four lung cancer and the loss of a mother, with whom she had a troubled relationship, feeling "guided by God" all the while. "I say to my students, 'Here's the key, open the next door. It's possible to have an intimate relationship with God,'" said Pell. "And they do."

Yet no matter what our mentors say or do, whatever they may ask of us, the choice to open that door and walk through it remains with each of us. The advice and experience of others can only take us so far on our spiritual odysseys. At some point, we have to strike out on our own and see where our own questions, our own intuitions, lead us. Each of us must stride or stumble down our own winding road, make our own mistakes, and by dint of self-examination, grow from those missteps. A guide is just that: it's up to each of us to chart our own spiritual course. There is a wonderful story from the Hasidic tradition about Rabbi Zusya. "In the world to come," he told his students, "they won't ask me, 'Why were you not more like Moses, leader of the Jewish people, or Rabbi Akiva, who died for his beliefs at the hands of Roman occupiers?' They are going to ask me, 'Why were you not more like Zusya?'"

As for photographer Lloyd Wolf, his journey would take him from his brief meeting with Heschel to a professional trip to Holocaust-era death camps and to Israel, close to two decades later. He would weather a painful divorce and explore Jewish themes in some of his eclectic photography projects.

One Yom Kippur, Wolf experienced an instant of inner transformation. During *Neilah*, the final solemn service of the day, he had fallen into a reflection so deep that it took him a minute to respond to his little daughter beside him. "I had dropped into a holy state, a sacred state," Wolf said. "My daughter tugged on my side and I reeled myself in." He suddenly grasped that Jewish practice had given him a healthier path to wisdom than the psychotropic drugs he had once taken in search of insight. "When I realized it was as natural as breathing, that was an important moment," said Wolf of the religious tools for renewal that he discovered in Judaism.

No matter how far his meditations, his travels, and his ever-present camera take him today, Wolf says he sees his long-ago encounter with a legendary rabbi as a touchstone for his Jewish life. "You know that phrase, 'What would Jesus do?'" Wolf asked. "I ask, 'What would Heschel do?'"

6 Scrolling Down
Encountering Hebrew and Torah

Hebrew was flying around the Chicago apartment as a dozen people swayed and prayed as if they had been born knowing how. The members of the Lomdim *chavurah* welcomed me with smiles and "Good *Shabbos*," but as a newcomer to both the group and the Saturday-morning service, I felt utterly, woefully lost. I could have faked my way through the liturgy, but a stubborn piece of my soul refused to pray what I could not understand.

On that Shabbat some twenty years ago, I bumped up against what, for me and many others on a Jewish path, posed a major impediment: Hebrew. Those seeking to reenter the Jewish world have to find a way around, over, or through the ancient alphabet, with its guttural consonants. Its vowels, largely spelled out in lines and dots above and below the letters, challenge the reader of English accustomed to separate letters for separate sounds. Hebrew also bears no resemblance to the Romance languages that some of us learned in school and, on top of everything else, is read from right to left.

Yet, practicing Judaism without any knowledge of Hebrew is a bit like trying to savor a gourmet meal without a full set of taste buds. Some of the flavor—and in the case of Hebrew, whole worlds of poetry, pathos, and significance—is lost. Adept in the jargon of science, biologist Jonathan Rosenfield has struggled with foreign languages. Hebrew, the idiom of Jewish prayer, has proved to be no exception. Language is one of the primary tools of Jewish religious experience. As Rosenfield said, "It's spiritual revelation by talking yourself into a frenzy." He also knows enough of what he calls the "sweeping, subtle, numerological" aspects of Hebrew to worry about missing shades of meaning, when the original Hebrew of Torah is translated into accessible, but less accurate and less evocative, English.

Hebrew—A Language Barrier for Some

David Abraham, a nominal Jew until he immersed himself in study and synagogue life five years ago, also points to Hebrew as a mountain he continues to climb. The sheer effort of following a service and the Torah reading, he says, holds back his understanding of Judaism. "It's still a very frustrating part of where I am in my own journey, my own education," Abraham said. "I would love to be able to read our Bible without an intermediary: every translation is an interpretation."

Like many others in pews across America, he spends services flipping between the Hebrew text and the English translation, without the ability to fully focus on either. And multitasking through the prayers makes it difficult to attain the sort of elevation he seeks. "It's kind of hard to get to a spiritual place when you're doing this Hebrew-English [translation] in your head," Abraham lamented.

Years before the doors of Hebrew opened for her, New York rabbi Judith Edelstein found that her ignorance of the language of liturgy made her feel isolated from the Jewish community. From her apartment window, she watched the parade of pedestrians carrying prayer books and *tallit* bags to synagogue during the High Holy Days. "Why can't I be one of them?" Edelstein had lamented. "Because I didn't know Hebrew, I didn't have the tools."

The very sounds of Jewish prayer deterred Debra Kolodny when she first ventured into the Fabrangen Havurah in Washington, D.C. After years of attending Quaker meetings, she was accustomed to the ripe silences and occasional utterances that typify this style of worship. "In all the clutter and cacophony of services, I felt lost," said Kolodny of her first exposure to Jewish communal prayer. "I wanted to shout, 'Don't you people know that God comes when you quiet down?'"

Kolodny enjoyed meeting people at the *chavurah*, but could not grasp the complex liturgy of the weekly Shabbat morning service. Yet, she felt drawn to High Holy Day services, where the melodies of Rosh Hashanah and Yom Kippur seemed to slip past her rationalist upbringing and sing to her soul. "The musical modes called up unconscious memory for me," Kolodny said. "I had never been at a High Holy Day service before, never heard that *nusach* [musical styling]. But it was in my bones."

For those living with disability, Jewish liturgy can pose special challenges beyond those faced by the able-bodied. Leslie Gordon was pursuing a graduate degree in Jewish studies at Berkeley's Graduate Theological Union when I interviewed her. That is no small achievement for someone living with cerebral palsy. At services, she struggles to balance a prayer book dense with Hebrew script in her shaking hands. "It's difficult for me to hold a *siddur* and because I don't say the prayers out loud, it's difficult to memorize them," said Gordon, forty-six, of Berkeley, California.

"My Soul Spoke That Language"

The same language, prayers, and texts that loom like a wall to some beckon to others. On a hike in New Mexico some twenty years ago, Albuquerque's Hershel Weiss met his first, inanimate Hebrew teacher. It was the root of a pinyon, a small species of pine tree indigenous to the American Southwest and Mexico, that he picked up on the trail. Soon, this woodcrafter was picturing it as a mezuzah, the long rectangular box enclosing a miniature Hebrew scroll, which is nailed to the doorframe of many Jewish homes.

Before picking up his tools, he sought to learn more about the three-branched letter that adorns this Judaic object. "What's interesting to me is that the act of making the object took me deeper into being a Jew: I had to learn what the letter *shin* was," said Weiss, who said that this project gave him "an appreciation of the power of the letters." He would go on to join a class on the mystical meanings of the Hebrew alphabet, which in turn enriched his experience of crafting other mezuzot. "Carving the letter *shin* hundreds of times, I developed a relationship with its mystery," Weiss said.

Seattle's Rabbi Tsurah August saw her Jewish education end with the death of her observant father, when she was eleven. Two decades later, she attended her first High Holy Day services at a *chavurah* on New York's West Side. Despite the language barrier, she felt an immediate sense of kinship with Judaism. "I didn't understand a word of Hebrew, but I cried during the whole thing—tears of joy," August said. "I had a sense of 'I am with my people.'"

One of her mentors, Rabbi Zalman M. Schachter-Shalomi, spoke of the "*sefer* [book] barrier" for some returning Jews. For August, surmounting that linguistic obstacle took both a shift in attitude and, on a practical level, hiring a Hebrew tutor to launch the Jewish education that would lead her to an adult bat mitzvah and, later, her ordination as a rabbi. "What I needed to do in my own mind was to change *barrier* to *threshold* because a *barrier* sounded impassable, but a *threshold* is welcoming," August said. "I could step over that threshold."

As a cantor-composer, Natasha Hirschhorn sees Hebrew text and liturgy in musical terms. "I think of it like overtones," said Hirschhorn. "You may not be equipped to hear all of them, but the more you study the language, the more you have access to these other layers of sound, of meaning." Take the word *olam*, which translates as both world and eternity. Hirschhorn points to *Melech ha-olam* (Sovereign of the world) and *olam va'ed* (eternity) as examples of "ever-expanding time and ever-expanding space, both within one word." Conversant in her native Ukrainian, plus Russian, German, and English, she finds in Hebrew an unmatched spiritual depth. "That makes it so mind-boggling and powerful, and I don't think there's an analogy in other languages," she said.

Judith Dack, who grew up in Baltimore, Maryland, among her mother's Syrian family, kept a distance from religion until well into adulthood. But her immersion seems to have prepared her for Hebrew. "Growing up in my family, I heard only Arabic words, the way some people hear Yiddish" alongside English, said Dack. Perhaps because she was grounded in a Semitic tongue, she experienced a sense of ease with Jewish liturgy when she encountered it again at midlife. "I found myself praying in Hebrew so quickly," Dack said. "I think my soul spoke that language already." She credits her ability to absorb its liturgical phrases to the chanting techniques she learned from Rabbi Shefa Gold. Dack has proceeded to take her comfort with the language into the Hebrew chanting classes she leads.

Meanwhile, daunted by the unfamiliar liturgy of Jewish services, Kolodny largely dropped out of communal life for several years until it dawned on her that a simple "skill gap" was standing in the way of a satisfying religious practice. She joined an adult bat mitzvah class at Fabrangen. As her Hebrew improved, the traditional Jewish prayers that had left her bewildered began to make sense. "I suddenly understood what the liturgy was about—that it was actually a very long and complicated meditation," Kolodny said. "And what better way to open up receptivity to God than to thank, bless, and praise God?" The pregnant silence of Quaker meeting had opened up a door to her spirituality, but she now realized there was more than one practical pathway to the Divine. "I decided that shutting up was not the only way," Kolodny said with a chuckle.

The Paradox of Torah

Beyond Hebrew and its prayers, the texts of Judaism can both attract and intimidate reemerging Jews. For some seekers, their own shifting interpretations of the Torah—read annually in most synagogues from start to finish—serve as spiritual markers, reflecting their inner growth. "The Torah portions change as you change," David Blumenstein said. "The more that I am doing my spiritual practice, the more I'm studying and involved, the more I see patterns." With the Hebrew he has mastered, biologist Rosenfield has grasped one of the paradoxes of Judaism's sacred writings. Their moral weight comes freighted with linguistic ambiguity. Multiple meanings are built into the language. The absence of vowels on a Torah scroll leave the words and the ideas behind them open to endless interpretation. "Change the vowels and you change the meaning," Rosenfield said. He now appreciates the layers of significance that can be uncovered in the Hebrew Bible if you read it, year after year, with fresh eyes. "Entire lessons are going on that are not in the linear sequence of the words," said Rosenfield, who has learned to find clues to interpretation in the structure of a biblical story, allusions to other stories, and subtle choices of words. For this seeker, exploring these "veiled" meanings of Torah remains a tantalizing pursuit.

Once a teen with a skeptical view of religion, Maggie Anton developed a passion for one of Judaism's most challenging texts. As her husband was burnishing his Torah chanting skills in preparation for the bar mitzvah he had never had as a boy, Anton signed up for a women's Talmud class. The experience set her on an unexpected course. "An astonishing thing happened: I just fell in love with Talmud studies," said this former secular Jew, fifty-seven. Not long after Anton started poring over these writings, she hatched the idea that would emerge, a decade later, as her novelistic trilogy, *Rashi's Daughters*. There was a legend, she learned, that the three daughters of the eleventh-century French Talmudist had worn *tefillin*.

Left with an empty house after her children grew up and moved away, the Glendale, California, woman was off on a quest to learn all she could about the Jews of a distant place and time. She turned to local university libraries in search of details on medieval Judaism. To her wonderment, Anton found references to women in the Middle Ages not only donning phylacteries, which were traditionally worn only by males, but also *tzitzit*, or the ceremonial knots on prayer shawls. Blowing the shofar and taking an *aliyah* (being called up to the *bimah* for the traditional blessings before and after a Torah reading), she discovered, may once have been open to both genders—an equality regained among liberal Jews in modern times and still elusive among more traditional Jews today.

Anton began re-creating the lives of her medieval peers. "I felt very connected to the women in this time period," she said. "It wasn't hard for me to imagine myself there, never mind the dirt and the bugs." One stunning insight drove both her personal exploration of Talmud and her writing of the novel: learning creates status. "Power in the Jewish community comes from knowledge; it comes from being able to interpret the Halacha [Jewish law]," Anton said. "I want us women to be empowered to take our seats at this table."

Secular-bred Debra Kolodny, who left the quiet of Quaker meeting for the more boisterous style of Jewish worship, now serves as executive director of ALEPH: Alliance for Jewish Renewal. As she studies for the rabbinate, she views religious texts that once might have troubled her in the light of history. "I watch my feminist friends get up in arms about things in Torah they feel uncomfortable with," Kolodny said. She shares their concern for women, but not their outrage: "My response is: For its day, the Torah was radically progressive." As evidence, Kolodny points to the "powerful women who are prophets, who have a direct relationship with God" and take charge of their families in the biblical book of *Bereishit* (Genesis). She draws inspiration from a story about the daughters of Zelophehad, who defy inheritance laws of the time that favored male heirs, by claiming family property after the death of their father. This episode in Torah, said Kolodny, "sets up the premise that God can change the rules."

As for my own journey, I did not stop long at Lomdim, the Chicago *chavurah* with the all-Hebrew services—despite the warm welcome and savory potlucks. It was just right for participants with a deeper grasp of liturgy, but not for me. Yet the experience whetted my appetite and led me to join a synagogue where I could learn the language of prayer more readily. Upon opening the *siddur* at the Jewish Reconstructionist Congregation in nearby Evanston, I found a window to a world of religious experience. Like a similar prayer book since developed by the Reform movement, it offered translations and transliterations that built a bridge to the Hebrew text for those, like me, who were unfamiliar with the prayers. I was back on my path, still climbing.

7 The Open Tent
Finding a Spiritual Community

A cultured New Yorker raised in a Yiddish-speaking family, doctoral student Norma Brooks felt clueless about Judaism when she first walked into a Boston *chevra* (friendship network). The group's acceptance soon put her at ease. "Even though I was really aware of what I didn't know, I felt embraced—I never felt judged or graded," said Brooks of her reentry into Jewish life three decades ago. "In fact, all of my doubts and questions were welcomed."

Untutored in the Jewish faith, with a mother who had disparaged religion, Brooks was amazed to find this community of intelligent, warm-hearted people who were equally committed to social justice and Jewish practice. Many also took part in services of Boston's Havurat Shalom, a local *chavurah*. "I had been told religious Jews were very divisive and arrogant," Brooks said. "Suddenly, I found myself in a world with really caring, bright people doing serious political and social work to make the world a better place ... but the thing that stood out for me was [that] they enjoyed being Jews." Brooks had walked into the right place to explore the spiritual side of her Jewish heritage.

A Communal Outlook

If it takes a village to raise a child, then it takes a community to build a Jewish life. Traditionally, the community rests on the minyan, or quorum of ten adult Jews needed to say the *Kaddish* and other key prayers. The custom of the minyan for mourners who are reciting the *Kaddish* after the death of a loved one guards against the isolation that can easily happen in the wake of deep loss. In a broader sense, a communal outlook is embedded in much of the liturgy of Judaism for Shabbat and festivals, from the *Shema* to the confessional liturgy of the High Holy Days. These prayers all speak in the voice of "we," the community.

When the congregational experience works, the individual seeker joins a chorus singing more or less in harmony. Joel Saxe makes his home in the Berkshires of western Massachusetts, but finding a Jewish service that meets his spiritual needs sometimes takes a foray to Florida. "They have a Saturday-morning service that will knock your socks off," said Saxe, of Reform Temple Israel, in Miami, the city where he's gathered oral histories of aging radicals for a film project. "It connects the ancient practices with contemporary ideas about social and economic justice."

The quest for communal spirituality has deep roots in Jewish tradition. Traditional Jews study Torah with a *chevruta*, or study partner. The ancient Rabbis spoke of the importance of human connection on the spiritual path. "Do not separate yourself from the community," the Jewish sage Hillel says in *Pirke Avot* (Ethics of the Sages).The Passover Haggadah goes so far as to consider a child wicked who speaks of the holiday meal in terms of "you," rather than "we," implying emotional distance from the other people around the table. And the Talmud insists on the principle, "All Jews are responsible for each other."

Such injunctions may speak to mainstream Jews, but people who have lived at the margins of Jewish life are still often wary of walking back in. The challenge of how to win their participation stirs perennial debate among Jewish communal leaders. A host of Jewish institutions, scholars, journalists, and authors have wrestled with strategies to appeal to unaffiliated or loosely affiliated Jews. In *Finding a Spiritual Home: How a New Generation of Jews Can Transform the American Synagogue* (Jewish Lights), for example, Rabbi Sidney Schwarz spotlights the strengths of congregations that succeed in drawing them in. In a thoughtful 2006 analysis, reprinted on the website beliefnet.com, *Jewish Week* editor Gary Rosenblatt called for the Jewish community to do a better job of listening to, rather than judging, the unaffiliated. He cites the story of Hillel, who patiently answered the skeptic who wanted him to explain Judaism while standing on one leg. "What is required of us is to emulate Hillel, opening our hearts and minds to those around us and speaking to their needs," Rosenblatt said. But he took issue with analysts who voice pessimism about the Jewish future. "Judaism is alive because it has been able to reinvent itself from generation to generation while adhering to its most basic tenets of *mitzvot* and memory," Rosenblatt writes.

Doors to the Tent

To get people into the door of the Jewish community, say the returning Jews that I interviewed, takes at least one of three things: a warm welcome, a connection to personal and social issues, and religious passion, which too often goes missing in synagogue life. It is a sense of embrace that drew Brooks to her Boston *chevra*, a message of relevance that brings Saxe to his Miami temple, and a spiritual enthusiasm that kindles sparks for others.

Emotional intensity attracted Judith Edelstein on her first visit to New York's Congregation B'nai Jeshurun two decades ago. "When I heard the cantor singing, I started to weep and I said 'this is what prayer is all about,'" recalled Edelstein. The secular-bred future rabbi found in the transliterated Hebrew a doorway to the liturgy and an echo of the social justice values of her childhood. "That was a major turning point ... the ability to pray, to feel a connection, and [to] feel my ideals revitalized," Edelstein said, recalling "a clarion call" to create a better world.

Even when a congregation has the strengths needed to draw alienated Jews back into the fold, it may take more than those initial attractions to hold them there. Jewish services comprise a kind of "graduate-level religion" obscure to many of those *davening* in a typical sanctuary, says Rabbi Hava Pell. Even the most familiar prayers cry out for interpretation, Pell believes: "Who's God? How do I love God? What does it feel like for me to love God?" She faults congregations for often failing to illuminate the ancient words of the liturgy so they can shine a brighter light on contemporary lives. "I don't see Jewish teachers breaking things down small enough so people can grow and change," Pell said.

Jonathan Rosenfield once commuted across Northern California for that kind of spiritual learning, driving more than sixty miles from Davis, outside of Sacramento, to Friday-night services at Chochmat HaLev, a center for Jewish spirituality in Berkeley. "This is not your grandfather's Judaism," said Rosenfield of the center, whose name translates as "Wisdom of the Heart." "There's music, singing, and not a heckuva lot of Hebrew." Initially drawn because an old friend was music director, Rosenfield stayed because something was feeding his soul. "I wasn't going there to have a Jewish experience," said Rosenfield, who grew up secular. "The religious tradition was not something I rejected, but something I didn't know much about." Now struggling to learn Hebrew, he finds Jewish services "joyful and deep." In his congregation, Rosenfield has discovered a "communal, emotional, spiritual connection" he never had before.

It's an unspoken truth of Jewish life that many people praying in synagogue harbor doubts about the existence of God, at least as traditionally defined. Sandra Lash is one of those. Though she remains unsure about a divinity, she joined a Reform congregation with her husband, Jeffrey. "I realized I had grown up with a lot of death and Holocaust and anti-Semitism and nothing else," said Lash, who directs a mental health clinic, adding, "I really needed to balance that; somehow my identity was skewed." At the urging of her rabbi, Lash began delving into books about her Sephardic heritage. This reading was her doorway into a broader sense of Jewish connection. Eventually, she assumed a leadership role in her religious community, serving on the board of her local Jewish federation.

Of Judaism, Lash said, "I like that it is not solely focused on a personal relationship with God, but on taking care of the entire community." She appreciates her tradition's accent on moral conduct and personal accountability. "There's a strong emphasis on leading an ethical life and taking responsibility for your behavior," Lash said. She points to this aspect of the religion as "something that's always resonated with me."

Judaism's Evolution

For Hershel Sakulsky, stepping into a synagogue after decades as a Jehovah's Witness was a Rip van Winkle experience, with a positive twist. "It's so good to be home," he said. "I walked into a synagogue, the temple I belong to now. I looked up and saw the *ner tamid* [the eternal flame] and felt God's presence." Sakulsky, who grew up among Reform and Orthodox relatives, was glad to see such traditional trappings as *kippot* and *tallitot* in the Reform world, along with a sense of religious relevance he had not encountered in his early Jewish experience. "Judaism has changed in the last forty to fifty years" for the better, noted Sakulsky, adding that he especially values the prayer book's translations, which invite him to ponder the deeper meanings of the texts.

In an era of scattered extended families and transient neighborhoods, Jewish congregations at their best provide a vital social anchor. When I interviewed Shirley Gould, she had already mapped out her ninetieth birthday celebration for the upcoming Labor Day weekend: lunch with her three children, her five grandchildren, and the minyan at the synagogue where she spends most Saturday mornings. "I've already reserved the kosher caterer," said Gould, a Skokie, Illinois, retired psychotherapist and author of several parenting books. Aside from her far-flung family, she explained, the minyan comprises the people closest to her heart. Since her husband, Joe, died eight years ago, friends from the Jewish Reconstructionist Synagogue of Evanston stay in touch with the spirited Gould. "If I don't show up at minyan on Saturday morning, I get a phone call," said Gould. "Nobody takes me for granted."

She remembers the congregant who helped her pick up her late husband from the hospital and took him to the barber for haircuts during his final illness. "This is a community that could be held up as an example," said Gould, who has belonged to other congregations and grew up among a vast extended family on Chicago's South Side. "It's really the first time in my life when I had that kind of support."

She and Joe joined the congregation after their children were grown and their former shul no longer inspired them. Thinking they no longer wanted to belong to a synagogue, they planned trips out of town over the High Holy Days. After two years of this, the couple reached a religious watershed. "By the time we got home, we knew we had to be part of a congregation," Gould said, recalling their drive to Skokie from scenic Starved Rock in central Illinois. "We couldn't shed it like an extra skin." The pair researched Chicago-area synagogues, assembled a list, and visited the Jewish Reconstructionist Congregation first. "Everybody made us feel so wanted and we liked the style of laypeople getting together to pray," Gould recalled. "We went home and tore up the list. That became our community."

A certain spiritual passion drew Pinchas Zohav to the first Jewish congregation he called home. In the early 1990s, he remembers line dancing on Yom Kippur to the prayer *Pitchu Lanu Sha'are Tzedek* ("Open for Us the Gates of Righteousness") with members of P'nai Israel, a *chavurah* in Charlottesville, Virginia. "In my dancing and my chanting, I had an experience beyond my norm," he recalled. "I can date to that redefining my relationship with Judaism." In this Jewish Renewal community, he found a kind of "experiential Judaism" that brought together the disparate paths he had traveled as the son of secular parents, a Talmud Torah student, a resident of Israel, and a seeker.

Zohav now belongs to two synagogues in the Seattle area— Congregation Eitz Or and Herzl-Ner Tamid Conservative Congregation—and sees the work of strengthening community as an integral part of the Jewish journey. "God spoke to us as a community at Sinai," he said. "Anything you do to support the Jewish community is a spiritual path—even if you go to a Passover seder once a year or order bagels and lox."

Lessons of Community

Communal life can add layers of meaning to religious practice, say many returning Jews. For Judith Edelstein, the *mitzvot* of Judaism have taken on new depth she never fathomed as a child, thanks to what she learned at B'nai Jeshurun. "The rules are relevant in that they provide you with a sense of holiness," she said. "Halachah is not an end in itself, but a means to a holier life." Over the years, as her Jewish ties have grown stronger and many-fibered, Edelstein has sensed an internal change that has accompanied her entry into the tent of community. "Before I came into Jewish life, I was more concerned with my own needs—my husband, my children, and me," Edelstein said. As she joined a congregation and ultimately, the rabbinate, her spiritual horizons broadened. "It's a larger stage now," said Edelstein, explaining her renewed sense of mission: "What can I do to create a sense of holiness for others as well as myself?"

Welcome, relevance, and passion may get seekers in the door of Jewish congregations and other community institutions. Emotional support, intellectual electricity, and the joy of shared holidays may keep them there a while. But the question remains: what does community offer on the spiritual journey that cannot be found by thoughtful individuals on their own? As I look back on my own Jewish evolution, the answer revolves around a shared sense of ethical aspirations. A spiritual community challenges me to be kinder with my words, freer in my giving of money and time, and broader in my focus, which, in the harried routines of American life, can easily shrink to self, career, and family. Watching mourners stand for the *Kaddish* prayer or hearing the names called out for the *Mi Shebeirach* (congregational prayer of healing) during Shabbat services provides a tangible reminder of the sufferings of others. In Jewish community, I am also surrounded by people, who, each in their own way, are striving to recapture some spark of the Divine in their lives. Their example helps guide me on my own path.

For one vision of community, we can look to Abraham, the biblical patriarch. Tradition has it that he pitched a tent open on all sides. On one occasion, God appears to him as he sits in the entrance, in the heat of the day (Genesis 18). When three strangers arrive nearby, Abraham rushes around to provide hospitality, involving his entire household in the process. He offers a bit of bread to the trio, but actually supplies them with fresh-baked cakes, cheese, and meat from a newly slaughtered calf. In this story, Abraham reaches out to strangers, anticipates their needs, and delivers more than he promises—not a bad paradigm for a congregation that works. The parable of the open tent also reminds us that building community is one way to encounter the Divine. Hospitality expands the soul.

8 Wrestling with Angels
Traditions That Chafe

Reclaiming Judaism often stirs up a mix of emotions—not unlike those prompted by an adult's return to a childhood home. Ask even those who feel the strongest pull back to their Jewish roots and you may hear reactions ranging from ambivalence to hurt and anger about certain elements of Jewish life. These individuals have committed to Judaism, yet they also find serious fault with aspects of the religion and the community they have come to love.

The name "Israel," given to the biblical patriarch Jacob after a night-long struggle with an angel, comes from a Hebrew word meaning "to wrestle with God." Indeed, grappling with faith, challenging God in the name of justice, and goading oneself and others to a higher moral standard all have deep roots in Jewish tradition. The patriarch Abraham, for instance, confronted God over his plan to destroy Sodom and Gomorrah. Though he lost the argument, Abraham set a precedent for arguing with God. Ancient prophets like

Isaiah—and not a few modern ones—have called the Jewish people to account for all the ways they have fallen short of their ideals.

In this tradition of dissent, aspects of Judaism raise problems for many Jews who are reclaiming their religious heritage. Women interviewed for this book tended to take issue with their treatment—or absence—in sacred texts and the religious roles assigned to women in traditional parts of the Jewish world. The men I interviewed were more apt to question policy and priorities in organized Jewry. Yet both men and women voiced anguish about divisions in the Jewish community over such controversies as the Israeli-Palestinian conflict and the status of gays and lesbians. Others raised concerns about what they see as unhealthy patterns in some Jewish families that drive people away from their roots in search of room to grow.

Reclaiming Women's Voices

Margie Klein, for example, is immersed in Jewish life and leadership from the communal Moishe Kavod House she coordinates near Boston—an informal center for young Jewish adults—to the trans-denominational rabbinical school she attends. Yet as she studies the words of rabbinic sages, she finds herself grappling with an age-old irony.

"There are times I feel like I'm in a dialogue with rabbis from two thousand years ago," she lamented, "and then I realize they wouldn't have talked to me because I'm a woman." Klein fought her own discomfort by researching and analyzing these Rabbinic sources for one of her seminary classes. "It felt subversive to become an 'expert' on these texts that said that I couldn't, or shouldn't, become an expert," Klein explained, "but also disempowering to know that the rabbis with whom I was in dialogue would likely have rejected me as a conversation partner, let alone as a *rav* [rabbi]."

Rabbi Leila Gal Berner is dismayed about not seeing women's experiences fully reflected in Jewish prayers. Herself a nationally known liturgist, Berner wrote "*Miriam Ha-Neviah*," which has found wide use at Passover seders and at *Havdalah* ceremonies, rituals marking the end of Shabbat. She also created "Our Silent Seasons," a ritual for healing from sexual abuse and abortion, adapted from the *Birkat Hagomel*, a blessing said after a brush with danger. "I shall bless the Source of Life / who fashions good and evil. / I shall bless the Holy One / who brings dark and light to all people. / For I have walked in the valley / of the shadow of death. / And You, and You / were with me then, / with every painful breath," reads part of the ritual. It echoes the rabbinic phrase *Eyn haChayim* ("Source of Life"); the *Yotzer* prayer after the *Barchu* call to worship, with its references to light and dark; and Psalm 23 ("the valley of the shadow of death"). Said Berner, "There isn't enough liturgy for women on these issues, and people are starving for it."

Although this Reconstructionist rabbi has found great joy in Judaism, she worries that Jewish girls still have to dig deep to find their lives mirrored in its holiest words. "Not to be able to point to women's voices until the modern era is very sad," Berner said, adding, "It's not so important that Leila Gal Berner's name is attached to it, but two hundred years from now, some little girl will know that women were part of the creation of Jewish liturgy, that our voices are there."

Like Berner, fifteen-year-old Hanna Switlekowski misses women's voices in the usual canon of commentaries on Jewish texts. "I also would love to see more Torah commentary by women, because as much as I love what the men are writing, there's nothing by women in the actual commentaries or the prayer books," she said, though recent *siddurim* (prayer books) from her Reform movement and another from the Reconstructionist movement are beginning to fill that silence.

Some contemporary women are busy reclaiming a piece of Jewish heritage that has troubled many feminists: the *mikvah*. Traditionally, Jewish women immerse themselves in the *mayim chayim*, or living waters, each month after menstruation. Recently, many women have turned to the *mikvah* to help heal from traumas such as rape and sexual abuse. Still others have used immersion in the ritual bath to celebrate a life passage, such as a birthday or a return to Jewish practice. Yet Margie Klein is not wholly at ease with the reasoning behind even reinventing the *mikvah's* use. "For me, there's a fundamental value I don't accept, that the body can become unclean because of blood," Klein said. "It seems like most of the activism around the *mikvah* gets people to participate in *mikvah* activities but doesn't challenge the assumptions behind it."

Faulting Faith and Culture

Some seekers take issue with elements that are deeply embedded in Jewish texts. Margot Barnet struggles with an idea from Judaism's core theology: the chosen people. She worries that this belief, enshrined in much of the liturgy of Judaism, runs the risk of isolating religiously serious Jews from other faith and ethnic groups in society. "Our tradition does not give us much help with how to live in a multicultural world," Barnet said. "If you think you have all the answers and other people don't, your ability to interact with others is severely compromised." Yet, on the plus side of the ledger, she also pictures the Torah as a "handbook for sustainability" for a tribal people in transition. In that light, it offers valuable guidance in "how to maintain sacred space when you're living close together."

As both a committed Jew and a serious yogi, Philip Mandelkorn raised a related question: do Jews obsess too much about who is a Jew, rather than focusing on what being Jewish really means? "People get so caught up in being

Jewish," Mandelkorn said. "It's sort of my football team versus your football team." Religions exist in a variety of forms, he believes, as systems to enhance wisdom and elevate the soul. He sees Judaism as a splendid spiritual ladder, but only one of several ways to connect with the Divine. "When you get to the top of the Jewish ladder, you're beyond Judaism," Mandelkorn said. Indeed, he believes, "you're in the same state as Catholics and Buddhists at the top of their ladder."

Once-alienated Jews tend to have a special empathy for those still estranged from Judaism. As someone who once stood on the outside of Jewish life looking wistfully in, David Abraham is frustrated by what he sees as halfhearted efforts by Jewish groups to engage Jews at the margins. He said he is "disappointed" that the organized Jewish community "doesn't have a very good ability to reach out to unaffiliated Jews and touch them." Now a vice president of membership at his Florida congregation, he hopes to work toward meeting this need in his own community.

If polled, some of the disconnected Jews on Abraham's mind would likely point to the high cost of Jewish life as a barrier to affiliation. The economics of Judaism are paramount for Joel Saxe, of Northampton, Massachusetts. A self-styled "eclectic Jew" with working-class roots, this former documentary filmmaker has followed his creative goals and never put the pursuit of material wealth at the top of his agenda. Now a media educator, he often feels alienated in Jewish settings where a middle- or upper-class income is assumed. He has felt "a constant ambivalence about wanting to feel connected, but feeling an outsider in the mainstream Jewish community.... The affluence of the Jewish community ... has brought a kind of materialism that's hard for me," Saxe said.

Does money hold undue sway over Jewish congregations and communities? A few of the people interviewed raised similar concerns. Ruth Kurlandsky of Fayette, New York, faulted the way that personal largesse affects how key decisions get made in communities large and small. "People who have money can say, 'I'll give ten thousand dollars and let's do this project,'" lamented Kurlandsky, who served as a religious school principal for congregations in Michigan's Grand Rapids area. "People who don't have money and say we ought to take on this project don't have the clout. That's the part about the Jewish community that annoys me."

Other people, both gay and straight, raised the mixed treatment of gays and lesbians in Judaism as a stumbling block to engagement. In recent years, Reconstructionist, Reform, Renewal, and *chavurah* congregations have welcomed gays as both members and spiritual leaders. The Conservative movement remains conflicted over whether to marry homosexual couples and ordain gay clergy. David Blumenstein, who has a gay family member, feels ill at ease with the ambivalence or outright rejection of gays and lesbians in the more traditional parts of the Jewish community. Citing the tradition of wrestling with God, the Virginia man reframes the parts of Judaism, such as the Torah's condemnation of gay men, that he can't reclaim. He has made a commitment to struggle with stands of his Conservative movement which he opposes, attempting to grasp their underlying values. "What I do is take seriously the existing positions, learn why and how they developed, and then wrestle with them, peeling back layers, trying to find the essence," Blumenstein said. "My goal is to find the truth even— especially—in things that I don't agree with." That examination may yield harmony or discord, but this Jewish seeker finds meaning in the struggle for understanding. "Sometimes I can find an alternative that is consistent with other principles, and sometimes I can't," Blumenstein said. "But I continue to wrestle, knowing that both the movements and I change over time."

Yiddish dance instructor Steve Weintraub, meanwhile, cannot help taking personally the traditional views of homo-

sexuality. He and his partner are welcomed at the Reform congregation near their home in a suburb west of Chicago, but
Weintraub's work takes him across the denominational spectrum of the Jewish world. In some quarters, he faces a lack of
acceptance. "As a gay person, I'm sort of living outside the
pale," said Weintraub, fifty-three. "Traditional Judaism does
not look kindly on gays."

Debate Turns Painful

Whereas social class and policies on gays divides some returning Jews in the domestic arena, others voice dissent about the
Jewish community's largely uncritical support of Israel. In
some circles, laments North Carolinian Bob Wineburg, this
political posture leads to quashing any criticism of Israel's
policies. "It's my country, right or wrong: if I don't believe that
about America, then I don't believe it about Israel," said
Wineburg, a Reform Jew. He rejects as "tribalism" the notion
"that you have to follow the line" on Mideast politics. Louis
Weiss shares his discomfort, pointing to human rights violations by both Israel and the Palestinians. He also worries
about what he sees as a damper on discourse among American
Jews about the Arab-Israeli conflict. "I have a hard time joining in with the Jewish community supporting Israel in an
unquestioning way," said Weiss, who lives in Chicago's North
Shore suburbs. "It seems like that's what's expected of
American Jews."

Meanwhile, several people I interviewed for this book
expressed concern about strife among Jews—the patriarch
Abraham's penchant for argument taken to extremes. This discord is a source of pain for many on their spiritual path,
including Diana Feygin, a Russian-American Jew who was
raised secular and is still sorting out her attitudes about
Judaism. "It is painful to see the deep rifts that divide Jews
along religious/secular lines, and even within the religious

world," Feygin said while on an internship with a Jerusalem think tank. "I have friends all over the spectrum, from *Haredi* [fervently Orthodox Israelis] to as secular as they get, and it is sometimes tempting to try to convince one side to reengage with the other in civilized conversation, though I know this is unlikely to happen."

As a poignant example, Feygin pointed to the 2006 gay parade planned to take place in Jerusalem, which ended up moving to a site outside the city after violent protests from fervently Orthodox Jews, which were augmented by outcries from some fundamentalist Christians and Muslims. At a similar parade the previous year, a man stabbed three participants. "It is so heart-wrenching to think that people can justify such hatred with claims to biblical truth ... that the same book that has given our people power and strength to survive so many atrocities can also fuel them to inflict equally terrible atrocities on their own kind," Feygin said.

Berner, too, agonizes over debates that have turned bitter in some corners of the American Jewish world. Such controversies as the role of women, policies about sexual orientation, denominational differences, and the merits of pursuing peace with the Palestinians have polarized Jews. She views these conflicts as the flip side of a quality she values in Judaism: "love of argument for the sake of heaven—*machlochit lashem shamayim*." From the days of the ancient Rabbis to contemporary times, Berner knows, Jews have argued over the best ways to live their faith. "On the other hand," she said, "one of the things that breaks my heart in Judaism is that we are so fractured as a people, that there are Jews who so despise other Jews that we can't even sit at the table and talk to each other."

As someone who has proudly reclaimed her identity on her own terms, Stephanie Ozer warns about the temptation to burnish Jewish culture to a romantic high gloss—seeing only its warmth, lively debates, and abundant comfort foods—without noting the darker side of Jewish families. Depression and other mental illnesses stalk many Jews. Anecdotal evidence suggests that a significant number grew up in families weighted down by pain, some of it born of persecution, from the vast shadow of the Holocaust to the scars of job discrimination and anti-Semitic bullying. "So many of us fled to the West Coast, to no kids, to other religions, or no religion, to renouncing our upbringings, to never going back to New York City, to not talking to our parents ever again, to marrying non-Jews to try to escape the suffocating sense of familiarity and transparency, the sense of no personal boundaries or privacy," said Ozer, a New Yorker turned Californian. With the wit and insight of Yiddish, for some Jews of Ashkenazi origin, came the psychic price of sarcasm and a certain emotional claustrophobia.

New York–born Pinchas Zohav, now of Seattle, fits Ozer's profile of Jewish transplants and shares some of her angst. He cites as a stumbling block on his own spiritual trek the splits and attendant judgments of one faction of Jews by another—"the divisions in our community that have us rejecting and not accepting each other." In his own practice, he aims to bridge those divides. "The challenge is really to embrace all Jews, all of Jewish experience and stand at Sinai for yourself," Zohav said. This returning Jew wrestles with his faith by striving for a balance between communal ties and the inward journey.

A participant in the renaissance of klezmer, the musical heritage of Eastern European Jews, folk-dance teacher Steve Weintraub also cautions about the nostalgic appeal of a culture both rich and flawed. He feels a sense of embarrassment about "that whiff of onions and schmaltz" emanating from "nebbishy, rundown, secondhand Judaism," even as he keeps alive its wedding dances. "We're trying to re-create and reanimate that" disappearing culture, Weintraub said. "We're glamorizing our Yiddish roots to some degree." From community strife and Israeli policies to gay and lesbian inclusion and the vestiges of discrimination against women: the more than sixty people I interviewed for this book harbor their share of discomfort with Jewish institutions. Indeed, the issues they raised have a familiar ring, since many of them surface in periodic surveys of the unaffiliated. Yet if Judaism's real shortcomings were enough to drive every questioning Jew away forever, I would have no book to write. Clearly, the people profiled here have mastered the art of living in a community rife with both holiness and human frailty. Their attitude recalls novelist F. Scott Fitzgerald's observation that, "The test of a first-rate intelligence is the ability to hold two opposed ideas in the mind at the same time, and still retain the ability to function."

Coming to terms with Jewish heritage, for the thoughtful seeker, means embracing a paradox: as Jews, we aim high, striving to be "a light onto the nations" (Isaiah 42:6, 49:6), and yet often fall woefully short of the mark, as we freely confess throughout the High Holy Days. To acknowledge and try to fix our failings as individuals and as a people is not to diminish the value of Jewish ethics, the power of Jewish ritual, and the grandeur of the messianic aspiration that, together, we can birth a better world. Indeed, it is the beginning of an adult spirituality, a path broad enough to have room for hope, healing, and contradictions.

II

Doors to the House

9 Generation to Generation
When Family Leads the Way

It took a daughter's spiritual thirst to bring Lou Weiss to the well of Judaism. Growing up in Steubenville, Ohio, Weiss saw the town's small Jewish community as a haven in a hostile environment. He recalls watching Ku Klux Klan crosses burning across the Ohio River in West Virginia. "I used to do my homework on the *bimah*" of the Conservative synagogue, said Weiss, now a child psychologist. "It was literally my refuge."

Then Weiss went away to college in the mid-1960s, and traded the verities of Hebrew school for protests in favor of civil rights and against the Vietnam War. "I didn't think all the rules and regulations that governed our lives were meaningful—the idea of keeping kosher and observing Shabbat, covering your head—the things that speak of a personal relationship with God," he said. Weiss kept his distance from Jewish life through marriage and the birth of his two children. At the precocious age of eight, daughter Rachel, now studying to be a Reconstructionist rabbi, told her parents that the secular

Jewish school she was attending was not meeting her needs. She yearned to study Hebrew, go to Sunday school, and have a deeper Jewish education.

Seeing synagogue membership as a "financial drain," Weiss and his wife reluctantly joined their town's Reconstructionist congregation, where they had friends. The first year there, Weiss experienced his own turning point during the joyous festival of Simchat Torah, when Jews the world over complete their annual reading of the Five Books of Moses and begin it anew. In the *minhag* (custom) of the synagogue, the children gathered in the middle of the sanctuary as their parents unrolled the entire Torah scroll in a circle around them. "Standing there, seeing the Torah myself, I was completely overcome with the significance of that," Weiss said. "I had an identity that belonged to me."

The Parenting Path

For many of Judaism's unmoored, becoming a parent precipitates their bonding with heritage. Some of these adults find reflections of their own childhoods mirrored in the faces of their children. In a paradoxical way, the illness or death of a parent or grandparent also can serve as a catalyst for rethinking Jewish spirituality at midlife.

That children often lead families to reconnect with synagogues and other institutions of Jewish life—through life-cycle events from b'rit milah (a boy's circumcision) and baby naming, to Jewish preschool and Hebrew school, to bar and bat mitzvah—should come as no surprise. That the renewal of these ties can have a profound, lasting impact not just on the children but also on their parents is less widely recognized.

Many returning Jews go through phases of rebellion as well as reconnection, but parenthood can catapult them into spiritual adulthood. When Chicago native Shirley Gould wed her late husband, Joe, as World War II was raging, the pair wanted to have nothing to do with their Jewish heritage. "We were going to have bacon and shrimp and anything we pleased, and we certainly weren't going to join a synagogue," recalled Shirley, ninety, of their early revolt against religion. Yet, the young couple's struggle to conceive the first of their three children led them to revisit that choice several years later. "She was quite a miracle," said Gould of Ruth (now Ruth Kurlandsky, also featured in this book). Ruth's birth led her relieved parents to revisit their religious identity. "We decided we were going to be positively Jewish," Gould said.

The Goulds took their first step by buying a menorah and lighting candles for each of the eight nights of Chanukah, a custom they maintained as their family grew. Shabbat dinner "with candlesticks, tablecloth, and the good dishes" became another household tradition, although the requirement to dress up for the occasion "caused some friction" with her children, Gould conceded. Yet she proudly recalls the comment by a young cousin who visited them one day. "How come when I come in here," he said, "I can tell this is a Jewish home? Mine's not like that!" Decades later, Gould can still hear his words. "That was how we raised the children," she said. The Goulds took adult education classes while their children in Hebrew School—including little Ruth—mastered the Aleph-Bet. "We were not asking them to learn something we were not interested in ourselves," Gould said.

Their first child, Ruth Kurlandsky, married a Jew but didn't set foot in a synagogue for years, despite positive girlhood memories. "At some point in college, I ate ham on Yom Kippur," Kurlandsky recalled. Yet when her first child was two, she and her husband, Larry, joined a Conservative synagogue. Otherwise, the Kurlandskys remained disengaged from Judaism until, on a whim, they attended a conference on Jewish education. It made religious educators out of both of them. The couple surrendered their old habit of going out on

Friday night, in order to be with their three children, light the Sabbath candles, and share a meal together. "We never became *shomer Shabbat* [totally observant], but we came from doing nothing, to doing it for them, to doing it for ourselves," reflected Kurlandsky. "The kids are gone now, but we still make *Shabbos*." She would go on to direct congregational religious schools, while her physician husband pitched in as a teacher.

North Carolina's Bob Wineburg, fifty-seven, grew up nominally Reform, but as an adult, cut loose from his religious moorings. "I hated Sunday school, Hebrew school, the whole deal," Wineburg said. Yet the birth of his son a quarter-century ago raised the issue anew. His non-Jewish wife, who later converted, insisted the boy be educated in some religion. They began with the local Unitarian church, but then the Reform movement adopted a policy permitting patrilineal descent. This suddenly made the Wineburg children Jewish—and led the couple to reconsider Judaism.

Reform Rabbi Fred Guttman "lit a fire in my son and we caught the fire, too," Wineburg said. As a minority in a strongly Christian region, this social work professor has reclaimed his Jewish identity in a way he never anticipated. "I can be an American citizen and do real Jewish stuff and be proud of it—in the Bible Belt," said Wineburg, crediting his rabbi for the change. "It's because he hooked my kids and I peeked in long enough to see what's there for me." He lights candles with his wife every Friday night and speaks of a new relationship with God and the Jewish people.

A veteran of a Hindu-style ashram and a 1970s rural commune, Jeffrey Kahn felt little connection with his Jewish roots until fatherhood flipped his world on its head. With his first wife, a lapsed Christian, Kahn broached a discussion about their kids' religious education as the youngsters were approaching school age, even though he was then largely estranged from his Reform Jewish background. Something pulled Kahn to give his two girls a Jewish upbringing. Recalling Passover seders at his grandparents' table as "an ordeal that went on for hours and hours," he sought to re-create a tradition for his daughters with more spiritual heft than he had found in his early years in Judaism. "I started doing this for my children," said Kahn, who ended up as president of his Vermont congregation. "I had no idea of doing this for myself."

Kahn still recalls a Chanukah party in the late 1980s as the congregation he later joined was getting organized. Suddenly, he was seeing Jewish traditions through his children's wonder-struck eyes, and it opened his own. "By the time I left that night, I felt a genetic tug that was so strong," Kahn remembered. "I saw my kids looking at the Chanukah lights for the first time in a Jewish community and I thought, I've got to do something. My children are going to be Jewish." Later as he built a life with his Jewish second wife, Rachel, the family began to incorporate Jewish ritual into the rhythms of their week. Rachel Kahn ushered in Shabbat by kindling the Sabbath lights. "When she began doing that, the girls and I were looking at each other and saying, 'Will we always be doing this?'" Jeffrey Kahn said. "And as it turned out, we would."

A developer of curriculum for the Jewish Reform movement, Joanne Doades grew up with parents who marked Passover with "matzah on the table" but nothing more in the way of ritual. "The Jewish gene didn't kick in, really, until I had children," Doades said, whose three children were born over a seven-year period. She now looks back to discover milestones for her own Jewish journey in that trio of births. "Around the birth of the first, I was ambivalent about my own Jewish identity," said Doades, who describes herself as "culturally" and "ethnically" Jewish at that point. To her surprise, her secular parents urged a Hebrew naming ceremony for that first child.

She assented to their wishes. As motherhood neared a second time, Doades herself planned a Jewish ritual. "By the birth of our second child, I had started taking parenting classes at the 92nd Street Y, so the Jewish side was strengthening," she said. "Soon after the second one was born, we joined the synagogue and were part of the Jewish community." For the third child, a son, Doades and her husband hosted a b'rit milah, or circumcision rite, at their home and participated in a naming ceremony at the synagogue. As her Jewish life expanded, Doades recalls a sensation of "stepping into a new world and getting my bearings." She and her husband now belong to both Reform and Conservative congregations, finding spiritual resources in both.

The Pull of Generations Past

For some people, picking up a Jewish thread requires reaching back a generation or two. Pinchas Zohav grew up in an assimilated family in the 1960s, but boyhood contact with his grandparents provided a loom on which he would later weave his own Jewish tapestry. "I could literally taste and smell the world my parents grew up in, the world described by Chaim Potok in his novels. I had Passover, bagels, and delicatessens," Zohav recalled. "It was through my experience of growing up as part of my grandparents' world that I absorbed much of the joy amongt the rituals of our Judaic spiritual heritage." He would later draw on those memories as he created a Jewish environment for his own children.

Yet Zohav worries that he failed to provide for his own children the sheer sensory richness of the Jewish life his grandparents shared with him, in a Bronx neighborhood marked by the rhythms of the Jewish calendar. "There is virtually no resemblance to my experience, no real sense of comfortable familiarity, no optimism that any future grandchildren will have a Jewish identity that looks anything like mine," Zohav said. For instance, he is now the only member of his family who knows how to make matzah ball soup. "I am left anxious, disconcerted, and wondering, have I thrown the baby out with the bath water?" Zohav reflected. "Have I unintentionally let them, my community, and God down?"

The death of a parent often touches off a period of soul-searching and reexamination of Jewish roots. A decade ago, the death of both her parents threw Ann Kline's life into upheaval. Her mother had a massive stroke; then Kline nursed her father during his struggle with terminal cancer. "Something happened in that whole experience where the dots got connected," Kline said. She recalled "an experience of love that was more than me, love with a capital *L*." Amid the pain of loss, she had a sense of enduring bonds with her religious heritage. "Losing parents, losing family, wanting a sense of identity—what did I have left but my Judaism?" said Kline.

Still unaffiliated at that point, she declined offers of a minyan to say *Kaddish*, because she would have been praying with people she barely knew. Yet she found meaning in the observance of *shloshim*, the thirty-day period of mourning. In a paradoxical way, this season of loss left her with a new sense of fullness, as she moved forward on a Jewish path. Since then, in the Conservative congregation she has joined, Kline has felt the power of the communal *Kaddish* as a participant in the *shivah* minyan (a group of ten or more gathered to comfort a mourner). "Availing myself of the gifts of the community and tradition now feels more natural," said Kline.

For Cathy Winick, the death of her beloved father three years ago was the final push she needed to commit to Judaism. The Grand Rapids, Michigan, woman comes by her religious heritage through her father's side. "I used to cook Jewish—boil bagels, make *tsimmes* [a stew of vegetables or fruits slow-cooked over very low heat]—the things my dad remembered eating as a kid" when she was a young girl, said Winick, who also recalled munching her way through family vacations in Hollywood Beach, Florida, where Ashkenazi standards from kreplach (meat- or cheese-filled dumplings) to poppy seed *hamantaschen* (pastry eaten during Purim) were served at local delicatessens.

Winick could walk into any Reform or Reconstructionist synagogue and be accepted as a Jew. A cultural Jewish childhood and patrilineal descent, however, do not satisfy the membership requirements for a Conservative shul, which is where Winick prefers to pray. "This is where my family would have gone," said Winick of Congregation Ahavas Israel. "I like tradition." She has mobilized books, tapes, and rabbinic support in an all-out effort to master enough Hebrew and religious learning for a Conservative conversion. "My dad was regretful that he did not continue the Hebrew education that his father wanted for him," said Winick, who calls her Jewish studies "homage to Dad."

It's a truism that parents live twice (or more), once through their own experiences, and again, as they meet the world through the eyes of their children. That opportunity to see the universe anew—to marvel at the breeze, the butterflies, or the sweetness of bananas—invites a sense of wonder and awe, good starting points for any spiritual life.

Some adults stop there, but others are impelled to delve deeper. For their own sake and for their children, they seek a framework that lends meaning to life's rhythms and upheavals, of birth and death, celebration and setback.

Among the first, and enduring, jobs of parenthood, after all, is to interpret the world for our children. Given time, young people will learn the mechanics of living, from using a spoon to driving a car. Yet, long after they have mastered the swing set, the gear shift, and technologies yet undreamed of, they will still need help making sense of a friend's betrayal, a neighbor's death, and the way that hurtful words (their own or someone else's) can wound as surely as bullets. Such Jewish values as shunning gossip, seeking forgiveness, and acknowledging blessings wherever we find them can help address the inevitable scrapes and disappointments of growing up. And as returning Jews bring to bear their spiritual resources on the moral dilemmas of their children, they have another chance at examining and healing their own.

In a similar fashion, the joys and challenges of child rearing or the pain of losing a parent tend to make people revisit their own beginnings and the families who raised them. These passages can kindle a renewed respect in people for the sacrifices of their own parents, along with the values that nurture them. As people grapple with a new sense of themselves as a link between generations, they are often drawn to a larger vision of life's purpose. Part of what it means to be fully human is to pass the wisdom we have learned to the next generation, be it our own children or those of others, as teachers and mentors know. The resonant phrase from Jewish liturgy, *"l'dor v'dor"* ("from generation to generation") only hints at the power of this process. As we have seen in the lives depicted here, this chain of transmission has the potential to move in both directions, surprising and changing us from the inside out.

10 Fiddler at the Door

The Arts as a Portal

Natasha Hirschhorn rediscovered her Jewish heritage in a song, or rather, in eleven of them. Browsing for new material one day, the Ukrainian native, then a musicology student at the Gnesin Music College in Moscow, came across a score that jolted her: "From the Jewish Folk Poetry," a Shostakovich song cycle yellowing in the library's stacks. "I was blown away to see the word *Jewish* on the cover in a mainstream library," recalled Hirschhorn, a pale, slender woman with a child's enthusiasm and an exile's sense of irony. In 1987, when she made her find, the Soviet Union was still repressing Jewish culture. Hirschhorn determined then and there to learn more about her lost heritage, kept alive on the pages of that score.

In recent decades, with surging interest in ethnic cultures of all kinds, many Jews have reclaimed their identity in a clarinet's wail, the brush of a calligraphy pen, and the raised arms of a dance. Using the tools of the arts—sound, color, movement, the spoken word, and craft materials from silk to wood—they are exploring questions of personal and communal identity. When Jewish text and ritual lie out of reach, whether because of oppression, lack of knowledge, or lack of personal affinity, people turn to the arts to find a way back into community life.

As for Hirschhorn, were it not for Shostakovich and his song cycle, she might have severed all ties to her religious roots. A Jewish college friend in Moscow was converting to the Russian Orthodox church, and Hirschhorn went as far as making an appointment with the priest. At the last moment, she called from a train station to cancel her plans. "I didn't really know why," Hirschhorn said. "It just felt uncomfortable, like the wrong move."

Her discovery in the library led her to study Hebrew, at first purely with academic research in mind. She joined an underground Hebrew class for Jews preparing to settle in Israel. "In order to join the group, there was this complicated chain of phone calls to be made," recalled Hirschhorn. She never learned the true names of the teacher or the other students; they all used Hebrew names. "I became 'Shoshana,'" she said.

Back in her hometown of Kiev, she pursued her new passion for the melodies of her people, joining the Kiev Jewish Youth Musical Theater, at first as a pianist. When her arrangement of the liturgical piece, *"Tov v'Salach"* ("Kind and Forgiving") proved too daunting for the group, she performed it herself—the first of many times she would sing in public and win applause for this additional talent.

Meanwhile, Hirschhorn found herself pressured both by the authorities, who were hostile to reemerging Jewish life, and by the fervently Orthodox rabbinic establishment, which frowned on women performing for mixed audiences. She determined to leave the country, applying for political asylum while in the United States for a piano competition. She remained here, eventually helping to bring the rest of her family to settle in the United States.

Over time, she found her niche in Jewish life as a cantor, a performing artist, and a Jewish liturgical composer in New York. Hirschhorn recalls "slowly realizing that I could have it all—I could be a Jewish musician and a spiritual person, and, eventually, a leader who could convey these two passions of mine to others." The young Ukrainian was mentored by Washington, D.C.–area cantors Sue Roemer and Sharon Steinberg before she went on to formal cantorial studies. Hirschhorn not only added the word *hazzan* (cantor) next to her name, but she also later became a liturgical composer with a national profile and a recording of her original works, *They Call Me: 9 Meditations on Hebrew Prayers.*

Today, when she brings her haunting soprano and improvisational piano accompaniment to the concert stage, Hirschhorn fields requests for non-Jewish music. But she remains committed to her own musical heritage. "People ask me, 'Why don't you sing lieder or outside Jewish music?'" Hirschhorn said. "I say, 'I don't need to.' In some way, I feel my voice is on loan for this purpose."

A Place in the Jewish World

For some, art can deepen Jewish identity and strengthen communal ties without necessarily renewing religious faith. Renowned klezmer violinist Alicia Svigals likes a synagogue with "real old-fashioned *hazzanes* [cantorial styling]," but her disbelief in God leaves her conflicted over religious affiliation. As a young girl riding to a violin lesson with her mother, she experienced what she describes as an atheist's revelation. "The clouds broke open and a ray of light shone down," she recalled. In that moment, Svigals realized, "There is no God. No one can read my mind. I'm free." Yet, the musician in her admits, to enjoying the melodies of Jewish prayer.

As a key player in the klezmer renaissance—she's a founder of the Klezmatics and continues to play this Eastern European genre at concerts and *simcha*s (joyful life-cycle events, such as weddings)—Svigals has seen this music function as a quasi-religious glue that binds younger Jews, who range from suburban refugees to current and former Hasids, to their heritage. "I feel like what connects most of these people is a pull to the world of our great-grandparents—a premodern way of life that for all its problems, was perhaps richer, less alienating, full of *communitas*, that people now long for," said Svigals, who earned a bachelor's degree in ethnomusicology from Brown University. Re-creating and improvising on the repertory of an earlier generation also cemented her bonds to the Jewish community. "If there hadn't been klezmer, I don't know if I would have found my place in the Jewish world," said Svigals, who identifies largely as a cultural Jew.

In the early years of the klezmer revival, as she and other musicians rediscovered the Yiddish songs and instrumental tunes of another era, they were gathering resources to feed not only their own souls but also those of others in search of their Jewish roots. "I was part of a small group of people unearthing a layer of Jewish life that was about to disappear," Svigals said. "I was trying to bring a whole Jewish lost city to the world."

Creating Jewish Moments

Other performing arts have also opened doors into Judaism for some of those pacing uncomfortably at the edges of the Jewish community, unsure of their place there. This proved true for dancer Steve Weintraub, of Oak Park, Illinois. Growing up secular in the Bronx and Yonkers, New York, did not leave him with much reason to cling to the smatterings of Judaism he had learned. "What practices people preserved, like fasting on Yom Kippur, were kind of severe," Weintraub said, while "the poetic practices that would draw you to the religion were left by the wayside." During college in the early 1970s, he was attracted to Asian spirituality and pulled away from his Jewish roots. "I'm not going to let a bunch of dead people tell me what to do," reasoned Weintraub, who practiced Transcendental Meditation for a couple of years. "I remember eating ice cream on Passover one year."

Through dance, he made a spiritual about-face. In the late 1970s, Weintraub bounded onto New York's Israeli dance scene, performing with the trio Rakdanim and later with the Parparim troupe, led by his mentor Ruth Goodman. "I discovered all this other culture through the Jewish dance world—Sephardic music and culture, Yemeni music and culture," Weintraub said. "I realized I didn't need Eastern religion. There was plenty of stuff in the attic that I could explore and draw from that was personally nourishing." Jewish history began infusing his choreography. He created "Scenes from a Spanish Haggadah," based on medieval book illustrations, and with longtime dance partner, Sharona Paller-Rubenstein, "Love on the Run: A History of the Jewish People Through Love Songs."

In his thirties, Weintraub shifted to a new corner of the dance field as the klezmer revival blossomed. Now an instructor of Yiddish dance, his work takes him from KlezKamp in the Catskills to Jewish family celebrations around the country. "When I go into a Jewish *simcha* [happy occasion] and I'm leading dances, I try to create a Jewish moment for people," he said. "At its best, it's ecstasy and longing. That's what you hear in the music and what you see in the gesture."

Reclaiming the Sacred

The closing decades of the twentieth century saw people of many cultures reclaiming their oral traditions. Among those exploring the spoken word were a host of Jews who brought the age-old art of storytelling back into the Jewish community. As they have re-created the tales of generations past, some find themselves rewriting their own life stories. Storyteller and children's librarian Susan Stone, for one, grew up in a traditional shul northwest of her native Chicago, where a bat mitzvah meant a small Friday evening affair without a Torah reading. As she became an adult, she realized that the roles for women in this Jewish community did not match her thirst for knowledge and self-expression. "I just didn't know how to be Jewish in a way that fit my life," said Stone, sixty, adding, "I love being domestic and baking cakes, but I also love learning and I didn't feel there was a place for me."

She practiced a minimalist faith, celebrating only the High Holy Days, Pesach, and Chanukah, until, in her early thirties, she picked up an obscure collection of Jewish tales of fantasy and the occult. Trained in the theater, she was tapped to tell her first (non-Jewish) story at a Halloween party. Word of mouth led to more gigs, as she gravitated to her passion: Jewish stories, which she began to study, record, and perform for area audiences. "All of a sudden, this was a way to combine who I was—a performing artist and a Jewish *neshama* [soul]," Stone said.

She was especially drawn to the tales of Hasidism, the eighteenth-century movement that accented emotional, experiential religion over cerebral text study. "It opened the door to spiritual seeking," Stone said. Preparing her performances, she delved into the countries of origin, the authors, and the cultures from which these tales emerged. And pondering their lessons has led her to look inward, to search her soul, to make sure that she can relate the stories with a measure of integrity.

This weaver of tales washes her hands before performing certain programs, especially around the High Holy Days. She also meditates in advance. "The Hasidic masters said if you tell a story with the proper *kavanah* [intention], it's as good or better than a prayer," Stone said. "Once I tell a story over and over and over again, it becomes like a mantra to me."

In recent years, the Jewish visual arts and crafts have flourished, led by the demand for handwrought Judaica in an effort to lend authenticity to Jewish rituals, celebrations, and home decor. Calligrapher Peggy Davis rode the wave of interest in *ketubot* that swept the Jewish world in the early 1980s. Her own girlhood was so secular that she recalls turning an oatmeal box into a Santa Claus figure. Today, this daughter of Marxist radicals makes her living from Hebrew calligraphy.

The Colrain, Massachusetts, artist, who is now fifty-seven, finds spiritual perks in her lettering work. "What's quite wonderful about it is it puts you in contact with Jewish texts," said Davis, who creates *ketubot*, invitations for Jewish life-cycle events, and inspirational plaques. She recently was thrilled to encounter a Talmudic quotation (*Yalkut Shemoni* 1:1) affirming that people of every color are entitled to their rightful place on Earth. "Most of the values my parents expressed—peace, justice, and human rights—I find them all in the Jewish tradition," said Davis, who leans toward a gender-egalitarian, traditional Judaism and belongs to a Conservative synagogue.

Healing Through the Arts

While the Jewish arts move some people from the secular world to an appreciation of the sacred, the creative process helps others heal the wounds of spiritual disillusion and alienation. Author, musician, composer, and teacher Louis Rosen recalls Passover seders of seventy-five people with his large, close-knit family during his early years in Chicago's South Shore. Throughout the 1950s, area Jews founded a Conservative congregation, built a synagogue, and then a Jewish community center—second homes for Rosen and other Jewish neighborhood kids.

Then white flight ripped apart this idyllic urban village as middle-class black families began to purchase homes there and whites put "For Sale" signs up on their lawns. Rosen sees the white reaction as fueled by a mix of racial prejudice, realtor pressure, and fear sparked by area riots. He watched the local schools' Jewish enrollment plunge from more than half in his eighth-grade class to a handful by the time he graduated from high school in 1972. His own parents remained in their home three more years, then moved northward to the integrated Hyde Park neighborhood.

For Rosen and his friends, the Jewish exodus undermined their beliefs as well as their neighborhood. "For many of us, the flight seemed to be a betrayal of fundamental teachings of Judaism to welcome the stranger," he said. He equated "the message of civil rights with the strong message that comes through the Passover seder, which is that slavery is a grave injustice and to treat your fellow man unfairly, to oppress, goes against the values of Judaism." He dates his estrangement from Jewish congregational life to that time.

Decades later, Rosen confronted his youthful sense of loss and disenchantment as he gathered oral histories from whites and blacks for his book, *The South Side: The Racial Transformation of an American Neighborhood*. "It was a personal journey for me," Rosen said. For years, he lamented, "I had carried around an anger about the Jewish community and its flight from that neighborhood." Meanwhile, Rosen had also composed *South Side Stories*, a song cycle in a musical theater style that gives voice to the Chicagoans with whom he grew up. He has performed it around the country with his musical partner, Capathia Jenkins, an African American vocalist. "What we are doing together is neither Jewish nor black, but informed by both experiences," Rosen said.

Through his writing and his songs, Rosen came to understand that the blacks who moved into South Shore simply wanted better lives for their children, much like their Jewish neighbors did. He also learned that some Jews had battled the tide of white flight and that others looked back on their choice to leave the South Side with regret. At a key moment, his childhood rabbi told him that children must learn that their parents have clay feet. "I suddenly realized that one must accept that and go on," Rosen recalled. "It was a relief—forgiveness without denying what happened, without denying the responsibility the community needed to assume." Though he remains ambivalent about Jewish ritual, Rosen recently joined a Reform congregation in Brooklyn, where he now makes his home. The book and the song cycle, Rosen said, "changed my relationship to being Jewish: I came to understand that a community is something one has to work for, fight for; we are caretakers."

Ask the best teachers how we learn and they will give you several true answers. Some people absorb every word on a page; others are avid listeners. Still others must tackle information hands-on, through doing. Another vital, but less well-recognized group of people learns best through their own creative synergy, such as a poem or a collage. Judaism has much to offer people with the first three learning styles: text study for the visual and cerebral among us, a dynamic *d'var Torah* or discussion for the aural learners, and the sensory richness of Shabbat and the holidays for those who must taste and touch the world in order to grasp its meaning. Meanwhile, the quest for religious wisdom often takes people in the fourth group, those who meld learning with art, in unexpected directions that can enrich both them and their audiences.

Dancer Steve Weintraub is the kind of person who takes a circuitous, but creative, path into Jewish life. His talent for choreography unlocked whole worlds of history and culture he otherwise might never have explored. As he said, the poetry of Judaism was hidden to him until, through his own dances, he uncovered some of the treasures of his tradition.

Frustration with the traditional roles of women blocked Susan Stone's full participation in Judaism, until storytelling opened another door to its wisdom. A consummate actress, Stone found a satisfying channel for self-expression in recreating Hasidic tales. In a deeper sense, the act of telling has forced her to reflect on her own conduct and consciousness. The Jewish values she brings to life through the spoken word, in turn, are changing her.

As for Louis Rosen, he found a way home to the Jewish world as he wrote a book and song cycle on the white flight that had shattered his illusions about the adults with whom he grew up. In time, the songs and the words brought him resolution, as he came to forgive his beloved Chicago neighborhood for all the ways it fell short of its best values.

A song, a dance, and the spoken word, among a constellation of artistic forms, can capture a bit of the magic of spirituality, sometimes when nothing else can. Artists become a channel for beauty and wisdom greater than themselves. And when this happens, the creators of Jewish art and those privileged to witness their work rarely remain the same.

Justice, Justice
Fixing a Broken World

Lenny Sapozhnikov walked into Judaism through the door of social justice. "For me, it was more of a portal into some organized Jewish life that otherwise I felt completely excluded from" by lack of knowledge, said the Washington, D.C., man, twenty-five, who was born in Azerbaijan. "The synagogue portal was a little too daunting."

Raised secular in what was then the Soviet Union, Sapozhnikov would find his Jewish niche in Jews United for Justice—a District group that aims to involve the area's Jewish community in work for social and economic justice—where he helped orchestrate a living wage campaign. Among Jews like Sapozhnikov, who grow up without much exposure to their religion, activism with a Jewish name can provide unencumbered access to their community.

The quest to define and establish justice leaps off the pages of the Torah and the writings of the prophets. "Justice, justice, shall you pursue," urges Deuteronomy 16:20, setting this as a condition for the survival and success of the Jewish people. Many commentators interpret the repeating words as a call to seek justice by just means. In the book of Amos (5:24), rather than demanding ritual without concern for social action, God says, "But let justice well up like water, / Righteousness like a mighty stream," as noted by Rabbi Joseph Telushkin in his book *Biblical Literacy*. Meanwhile, the Hebrew Bible is peppered with references to the fair and compassionate treatment of the dispossessed—the widow, orphan, and stranger, in the parlance of the times.

Even for Jews who have never glanced at these texts, social-justice work can serve as an easy and intrinsically valuable path into the community, free of the language barrier of Hebrew and the conventions of Jewish worship that may intimidate Jews who are not steeped in their own tradition. Books like *Judaism and Justice: The Jewish Passion to Repair the World* (Jewish Lights) by Rabbi Sidney Schwarz and *Righteous Indignation: A Jewish Call for Justice* (Jewish Lights), edited by Rabbi Or N. Rose, Jo Ellen Green Kaiser, and Margie Klein, illumine at greater depth the drive to build a more equitable world that powers much of the Jewish tradition. And, as we will see, that portal to a Jewish journey often, if not always, leads to unanticipated spiritual destinations.

"A Comfortable Door"

Growing up, Sapozhnikov knew he was Azeri, but his notion of being Jewish was somewhat hazy. "Lenny, Lenny, Leonid / You're not a goy, but a Yid," his father would sing to him when he was little. The boy's maternal grandfather, a Communist Party stalwart, would stop by the Baku synagogue to pick up his matzah for Passover. At ten, Sapozhnikov left the country with his family for Brooklyn, where they briefly lived alongside what seemed to him the "entirely alien" culture of Hasidic Jews. After a traditional Pidyon HaBen (a ritual that redeems a firstborn son from dedication to God), at the urging of their new neighbors, the family fell back into secular life.

The redeemed firstborn turned his attention to math and karate. Later, during college, other students exposed Sapozhnikov to Eastern philosophy. He spent some time visiting a chi gong community, but the Asian traditions didn't fill his spiritual glass. "I felt it was premature to fulfill that spiritual hunger through the Eastern traditions—before taking the time and exerting the effort to dig deep in my own Jewish tradition," Sapozhnikov said. His curiosity prompted visits to Hillel services at George Washington University, where he was studying. "I tried Orthodox services downstairs and Conservative services upstairs," recalled Sapozhnikov, who felt alienated by the Hebrew and the liturgical sequence he didn't yet grasp. "I kept going, while, frankly, not finding it as fulfilling as I wanted it to be." He shopped for shuls across the District's Jewish spectrum, from Orthodox to Reform to *chavurah*-style, without finding the right spiritual home.

Then a brief trip to Israel, taken with a skeptical eye, allowed him to spend time with his paternal grandparents, who had settled there. Their conversations filled in some gaps in his family's history. "I guess I was looking for evidence that we weren't Jews in name only," said Sapozhnikov. Indeed, his grandmother told him that her own mother lit Shabbat candles and cherished a *chumash* (a Hebrew Bible with the Five Books of Moses and some prophetic writings).

Upon his return, Sapozhnikov plunged into Jews United for Justice. "For me, for a while, being Jewish meant running a JUFJ campaign," said Sapozhnikov, who led the organization's successful living-wage drive and eventually joined its board. "It was a comfortable door."

Torah as a Call to Justice

Others have entered Jewish life through the study of sacred texts only to discover a passion for justice as they learn. Barry Leff's more roundabout route into activism began with a midlife reconnection with religion, sparked by his wife's conversion to Judaism. His journey ultimately led him into the rabbinate. It also prompted him to give new weight to *tzedakah* and to bettering the world. He serves on the executive board of Rabbis for Human Rights (RHR), an advocacy group that addresses alleged rights violations in Israel and the United States. "I really was not passionate about social justice issues until getting into Torah," said Leff, adding, "I certainly give more money to charity and give more time to groups like RHR than I did before."

He and his family made *aliyah* to Israel last summer, another leg in a still unfolding journey. "The State of Israel is clearly the most exciting thing to happen to the Jewish people in two thousand years, and I want to be a part of it," said Leff, before moving. "In addition, it's really important that we get it right." He wants the Jewish state to reclaim its mission of *or l'goyim* ("a light unto the nations") in the arena of human rights.

Leff attributes his new passion for justice to learning about the mystical interpretation of *tikkun olam* (repairing the world) by sixteenth-century mystic Isaac Luria. He taught that, in the beginning of the world, the Divine Self contracted to make space for creation. Divine light was gathered in *kelim* (sacred vessels). Some of these shattered, and their shards dispersed the light. To mend the damage, according to Luria, human beings must carry out *mitzvot*, holy deeds. In recent decades, many Jews have interpreted this as a mandate for social justice.

Toward Healing the World

For others, social justice is a boulevard. In one direction, this divided road leads into Judaism; in the other direction, it leads toward a wider horizon that includes the non-Jewish world. This matches the experience of Simon Greer. "As I proceeded along my social justice journey, I was moved, inspired that Judaism taught that you have to heal the self and the soul, and the system and the world at the same time," Greer said, citing the twin Jewish values of *tikkun olam* and *tikkun hanefesh* (healing the soul). The son of Orthodox-raised parents turned secular—poor Londoners who rose to affluence—Greer helped found Jews United for Justice in Washington, D.C. He is now president and CEO of Jewish Funds for Justice, a New York–based philanthropy that makes grants to grassroots groups that address social and economic inequity in the United States.

For Greer, such causes are like a door swinging open in both directions. "A really authentic Judaism has justice at its core," said Greer, who tends to spend his Saturday mornings out in nature rather than at a synagogue. "In my life, social justice was a way back into Judaism ... and an animating force to go back out to the broader community."

Judaism and justice came as a package for Greer when he was growing up. His immigrant parents taught him compassion for those left outside the circle of prosperity. From his mother, he heard the message: "we should love America because this [good life] is possible only in America, and we should be angry that the journey is out of reach for so many others." Solidarity with the oppressed was reinforced at Camp Kinderland in Massachusetts, a summer program founded by the Workmen's Circle (Arbeter Ring). His bunk bore the names of civil rights martyrs James Chaney, Michael Schwerner, and Andrew Goodman. Greer shared New York roots with the latter two. "I noticed that Andrew Goodman went to the same grammar school, the same high school," Greer recalled. "I thought that dying for civil rights was what Jews did."

After college, Greer moved to Poland to work with the youth division of the Solidarity trade union. The experience opened his eyes to the potential and limits of social transformation. "Everyone I met was part of changing that country," Greer said. "It didn't matter if they were a priest, an office worker, a teacher, or a shipyard worker."

Meanwhile, he also felt a growing interest in his Jewish heritage, which had been largely excised from Poland during the Nazi occupation. "Living in Poland, I suddenly felt more attached to it, more scared—not wanting to be anti-Catholic, but pro-Jewish and feeling I didn't know enough to know what pro-Jewish looked like," Greer said.

In the mid-1990s, Greer shifted to a new arena: community organizing in North Carolina. He met no other Jews in the area. As part of his work, Greer would attend black Baptist churches on Sunday, where he would sometimes be asked to preach. At a virtual loss for words, he resorted to talking about the Exodus story he had learned at Passover seders. In 1995, he says, when area white supremacists tried to blow up a church where his organization met, he sensed "a meanness rising in me" in response to a brutal opposition. Greer also realized successes, as when the rural bus drivers there won their fight for better working conditions. It reminded him of Nachshon ben Aminadav, the first Hebrew to set foot in the Reed Sea while crossing out of Egypt. "In that moment, I understood what they were doing—their courage, their bravery—through a Jewish lens," Greer said. "Somehow I had gleaned from Pesach that this character, Nachshon, stepped out toward the Promised Land, rather than return to slavery."

The idea of *tikkun olam* that spurred Greer and others to leadership in the justice arena has gone mainstream. You can hear the term bandied about by leaders across the Jewish establishment. In the process, some activists worry that the Jewish insistence on social justice could be losing its prophetic punch. "That teaching, to heal the world, is a call to action," Greer lamented. "To reduce it to bringing one can of food or [writing] a thirty-six-dollar check shies away from the power of that call."

He is not alone in his concerns. Activist Margie Klein faults what she calls "feel-good" *tikkun olam* rhetoric—unmatched by deeds that challenge injustice. "The person of faith can't look at the world and only see what's realistic," Klein said. "The person of faith needs to believe [that] when people come together and join their collective power, the possibilities change." She has witnessed this transformation many times—in her work with disenfranchised groups in Boston, Latino immigrants with whom she traveled in a 2003 cross-country Freedom Ride, and politically concerned college students she rallied through Project Democracy, a group she founded in the run-up to the 2004 elections.

What can be seen as hackneyed references to *tikkun olam* may also obscure the web of motivations—secular and religious—that have historically drawn Jews to social justice work in disproportionate numbers. Greer points to Jewish engagement in the black civil rights movement of the 1950s and 1960s as a telling example. Some Jews who joined this cause saw the oppression of blacks through the Marxist lens of class struggle. Others identified with the civil rights movement because their families had felt the sting of discrimination in jobs, housing, colleges, or country clubs. A third group, represented by Rabbi Abraham Joshua Heschel, drew inspiration from the Jewish prophetic tradition. "It's important that Jewish involvement in social justice has always had multiple strands," Greer said.

Rabble-rousing and Religion

Some people come to build lives that meld social causes and spirituality, forging communal ties through their activism that lead them to reclaim Judaism. Jewish farmer-activist Mike Tabor, of Takoma Park, Maryland, followed such a path. Growing up "Conservadox" in Brooklyn and Queens, Tabor traded in Judaism for rabble-rousing. "My favorite thing to do on the High Holy Days was to walk over to Union Square and watch the revolutionaries on their soap boxes," said Tabor, who now attends *chavurah* services during the Days of Awe. Close to his maternal grandmother, who ran a newsstand on the Lower East Side, Tabor recalls her house full of *pushkes* (small containers for collecting money for philanthropies) and her tales of fruit orchards in what's now Romania. From this contact, he developed a "deep attraction to *Yiddishkeit* [Jewish culture]," Tabor said, yet "the religion was always boring, inconsistent, or irrelevant to me."

Upon moving in 1963 to Prince Georges County, then a largely white suburb of Washington, D.C., for a doctoral program, Tabor went out for a beer with a black friend from the North. They could not get served together at a local bar, due to the region's prevailing segregation. That experience drove Tabor to join antisegregation protests with Congress of Racial Equality (CORE) and Students for a Democratic Society (SDS). The young activist observed members of his own community playing roles on both sides of the struggle. For "an awful lot of the white activists, the thing we had in common was being Jewish," Tabor said. Yet he was also disturbed and shocked by the discriminatory practices of some Jewish real estate owners. "That so many slumlords and segregationists were Jews didn't make any sense to me at the time," Tabor recalled.

Meanwhile, a question from a black activist about Tabor's heritage prompted him to grapple with his own identity, even while fighting for the rights of others. He helped found Jews for Urban Justice (1966–71) to create an explicit Jewish presence in Washington's civil rights movement. Out of that group grew Fabrangen, the *chavurah* to which the mystically inclined but still politically active Tabor belongs today.

An increasing number of younger Jews in newer institutions such as Jews United for Justice and the Moishe House network are melding the imperative to change the world with religious values. Margie Klein is seeing that fusion work at Moishe House Boston: Kavod Jewish Social Justice House, a center of Jewish life for young adults in the suburb of Brookline, Massachusetts, which she coordinates. "People are hungry for a kind of Judaism that is engaged with the world, that embodies powerful values," Klein said, "because it gives us strength and it grounds us in a long-term redemptive vision." Greer has a slightly different reading of trends. As he travels around the country for the Jewish Funds for Justice, he senses from Jewish audiences both a weariness with conventional rhetoric on justice issues and a hunger to put Jewish ideals into action. "I hear a fair amount of resistance or skepticism about the words *social justice, tikkun olam,* and *tzedakah,*" Greer said. "When we talk about effective expressions of Jewish values, I hear a lot more resonance."

Social justice can be a satisfying way to reconnect with the Jewish community, even for those who do not make it their full-time job. When Lou Weiss joined a synagogue, at his daughter's instigation, he was drawn to such projects as feeding the homeless and helping a Guatemalan refugee family get on its feet in the Chicago area. As he gradually deepened his involvement, Weiss was "realizing that in college, I had rejected Judaism for social action and I could readopt Judaism and be involved in social action from a Jewish point of view." In Miami, lawyer David Abraham finds the biblical teachings about human dignity resonate with him, and feels driven to work on behalf of community groups, on top of his legal practice. Through his wife's work in interior design, he came into contact with the gay community and has offered his skills to gay rights groups. "Ours was the first tradition to say that the laws apply to all people—not just the powerful and the rich," Abraham said. "The Ten Commandments were given to everybody, even non-Jews; men and women were together at Sinai." For Abraham, the justice messages of the Torah and the prophets trump a few verses in Leviticus that proscribe gay male sex.

Many Jews—from the staunchly secular to the deeply, if not always traditionally, observant—see social justice at the forefront of their identity. Rooting his activism in Jewish soil, Tabor turns to the wistful words of a young girl who was writing in the shadow of the Holocaust she would not survive. "It's a wonder I haven't abandoned all my ideals, they seem so absurd and impractical," wrote Anne Frank from her Amsterdam hideout in July 1944, weeks before her family was sent to Nazi extermination camps. "Yet I cling to them because I still believe, in spite of everything, that people are truly good at heart." That kind of hope in the face of social evil grounds Tabor's spirituality today. "There is a certain naiveté to this, but I'd like to think that all people have an inclination to do good," Tabor said. "If that's the case, there might be a force in the universe that dictates goodness rather than evil."

For her part, Klein reads meaning in the Sabbath *Kiddush* prayer—which links the day's respite from work to the Israelites' liberation from Egyptian bondage—that has illumined her discussions with activist friends since her college days. "We tried to use Shabbat to think about exodus from *mitzrayim*, from the narrow places in our lives," said Klein, citing the Hebrew word for both Egypt and straits. Such weekly conversations have sustained Klein and her allies on the bumpy, meandering road to a better world. "You can get so mired in the problems that you forget what you're working for," Klein said. "You're so much in the desert that you don't even remember the Promised Land."

Activism as a Bridge

The social justice path can sometimes lead to fuller participation in the larger Jewish world, including religious life. For Sapozhnikov, becoming a leader in a group like Jews United for Justice led him to explore other parts of his Jewish self. Pointing to the three pillars of Judaism—Torah, service, and lovingkindness—he says he is now pulled to begin serious work on the first two. "If I entered Judaism through the social justice portal, then I'm now finding myself hungry for those two other pillars," Sapozhnikov said. "I'm finding myself more interested in study, prayer, and contemplative practices." As a catalyst for learning, he teamed up with his twelve-year-old brother for a bar mitzvah last summer. "I really enjoy that self-enforced commitment," he said about the preparation for the ceremony. But for Sapozhnikov, the spiritual road winds into uncharted terrain. "I'm still unclear where this is going," he said.

Most of the people profiled in this chapter have focused their *tikkun olam* on curing social ills—racial and economic injustice—that afflict the United States. Yet many others, fired by traditional Jewish mandates of solidarity with other Jews and empathy for the most vulnerable (Jewish or not), have championed causes that span the globe. In the 1980s, American Jews marched in support of their brothers and sisters in the Soviet Union, who for decades could not express their faith and culture, or leave the countries that oppressed them.

Still other activists have mobilized to halt the genocide of hundreds of thousands of people in the Darfur region of southwest Sudan. This movement has united Jews who are generations apart—from college students to Holocaust survivors—and drawn the support of major Jewish organizations. Decades from now, some of those currently picketing the Sudanese embassy, lobbying their lawmakers on Capitol Hill, and writing Talmud-inspired blogs on the genocide, may look back on these efforts, worthy in themselves, as a bridge they walked into a larger world of Jewish values.

12 Communal Callings
Serving the Jewish People

Barry Leff spent a quarter-century sprinting up the executive ladder in the high-tech field, rising to become vice president of marketing for a semiconductor company. A veteran of Army intelligence with a pilot's license and a black belt in karate, Leff was accustomed to excelling, but his wife's conversion to Judaism changed the focus of his ambition. He starting delving into Jewish texts and took their words to heart. "When I studied Torah and fell in love with it, I came to realize that it was about making the world a better place," said Leff, now a Conservative rabbi. "It wasn't about making money."

For a surprising number of late-blooming Jews, the road to inner growth has led to careers in the Jewish community, as clergy, educators, and professionals. Many more have found fulfillment as staff members and lay leaders of congregations, local federations, and other communal institutions. In conversations with both groups, the motif of "meaning" surfaces frequently. Having sampled other work or volunteer vocations, they speak of wanting to contribute to something bigger than their own professional success, economic security, and family's well-being.

Drawn to Inner Space

Prior to his continuing romance with Torah, Leff, fifty-one, claims he only set foot in synagogue three times in two and a half decades, once for his brother's bar mitzvah and twice for weddings (not his own). Yet he also recalls "exploring inner space" as he devoured books on Buddhism and experimented with meditation in his twenties. Judaism did not seize his attention until he read *The Jew in the Lotus* by Rodger Kamenetz and became aware of Kabbalah, the realm of Jewish mysticism. "To find spiritual depth and meaning in something that felt culturally familiar was great," Leff said. "What opened the door was the Kabbalistic concept of God as *Eyn Sof* [Infinite]."

Undaunted by his sparse knowledge of Hebrew, he embarked on a course of Daf Yomi, a program for reading the entire Babylonian Talmud over seven and a half years, at the relatively hectic rate of one two-sided page a day. He enjoyed probing, albeit in English translation, through layers of rabbinic debate and interpretation—what he calls "intellectual archaeology." With that accomplishment behind him, he quit his corporate job and headed for rabbinical school.

A congregational rabbi in Toledo, Ohio, when interviewed, Leff is still digging up buried treasure in Jewish texts. After spending twenty-five years in what he calls "the spiritual wilderness," he wants to share what he's learned. "I love going through Torah and finding teachings and values that are incredibly relevant to problems and lives today," Leff said.

Taking on Jewish spiritual leadership later in life gives him both a twinge of regret and a sense of confidence. He has a routine of studying on Shabbat afternoons with his daughter, eleven, who attends Jewish day school. "With the head start she's got, she'll learn more Torah than I'll ever know," Leff said. "On the other hand, the life experiences I had really contribute to my effectiveness as a rabbi because I can relate to the congregation in a much deeper way." After all, he notes, he used to sit on the other side of the sanctuary, as a congregant. Like many seekers who spent years on the margins of the Jewish community, he brings a natural empathy for those still on the outside, looking through the windows, reluctant to walk in.

Serving as Interpreter

Jewish clergy from secular backgrounds can take their enthusiasm for the spirituality they found as adults and help interpret Judaism to others still on the journey home. Leila Gal Berner's first steps into a Los Angeles synagogue took her far down the road of religious commitment. In short order, she went from being an unpaid service leader to a serious student of Judaism and opted to research thirteenth-century Barcelona Jews, instead of medieval church history, for her doctoral dissertation. "My eyes were opening to the fact that this religious tradition is incredibly rich," Berner recalled. "I realized that there was this whole world and I wanted to learn all of it."

While serving on the search committee for her congregation's first rabbi, Berner began thinking about entering the clergy herself. She turned down a tenure-track professorship to attend the Reconstructionist Rabbinical College. Just thirteen years after first setting foot in a synagogue, she was ordained as a rabbi. "My heart and soul and mind have many different rooms, but most were closed; but when I began to discover spiritual Judaism, all these doors started opening," said Berner. "I didn't have to live only in the world of the intellect." As she once dreamed, Berner has dual careers, with a rabbinic post at Kol

Ami: The Northern Virginia Reconstructionist Community and
adjunct professorships at George Washington University and
American University. She also directs Lev Tahor: A Center for
Jewish Soulwork, which she founded to promote spiritual
direction in the Jewish community.

As one who has crafted liturgy herself, Berner finds fulfillment in making the world of prayer accessible to others. Many
Jews, she contends, come to services needing a bridge to the
Hebrew liturgy, such as a poem or meditation. Marshaling the
words that will help them make the crossing from contemporary lives to ancient imagery presents, for her, a "creative
process" and a satisfying challenge. "When it works, I can
sense it in the energy in the room, when people come in tired
on a Friday night or just waking up on Saturday morning."
The building of that spiritual momentum recharges her as
well. "I often come to services tired, and almost always I am
more energized afterward," Berner said.

A religious reentry at midlife can forge a stronger spiritual
leader, say some second- and third-career clergy. People who
recommit to Judaism after half a lifetime doing other things
often bring not only renewed passion but also hard-won wisdom about the obstacles to faith. For two decades, Shafir
"Candy" Lobb was a "private Jew" who called herself "spiritual, not religious." The daughter of a Conservative rabbi with
an Orthodox *s'micha* (ordination), she aspired to follow his
path at a time when the Conservative movement was not
ordaining women and the Reconstructionist Rabbinical
College, which she briefly attended, felt inhospitable to Lobb.
"I backed off from a dream and went to my brother's ordination," she recalled.

A warm welcome at two synagogues when she was mourning her mother's death provided this alienated Jew with another
chance to explore her religious heritage. She went on to pursue
rabbinic ordination in the Jewish Renewal movement and now

serves an Arizona congregation. Today, Lobb looks back on her personal setbacks as training for her current career. "Had my path been that of a conventional rabbi, I would not have had the proper empathy for the dual world that the rest of the Jewish world lives in," Lobb said. "I think that spiritual leaders do their best work growing through their pain."

A Volunteer Vocation

In the unglamorous but necessary work of governing Jewish institutions, many others find a way to contribute and to grow. Retired teacher Dottie Bennett, sixty-six, of Falls Church, Virginia, has found her Jewish calling in lay leadership. Born in New York of German and French refugees from Nazi-occupied Europe, she grew up without much in the way of Jewish practice. Yet her adult experience of raising a Jewish daughter in an interfaith marriage spurred Bennett's efforts to learn more about the religion that her assimilated family had largely shelved. "I became more knowledgeable as she did," Bennett said of her daughter, Ann, now a mother herself. "She remained my inspiration."

Moving to northern Virginia in the late 1960s offered Bennett her first lay leadership challenges. Aside from a handful of synagogues, the region had little in the way of Jewish life. "It was a really meaningful opportunity, to get in on the ground floor of building a Jewish community," said Bennett, who with others helped develop the Jewish Community Center of northern Virginia, the first such institution in the region. As she grew into local leadership roles, Bennett found in Ambassador Al Moses, a past president of the American Jewish Committee, a mentor who helped her hone her skills for larger arenas. From Moses, she gleaned an important lesson, that "Jewish learning was an integral part of leadership." The nub of his advice, Bennett said: lead not from the organization's mission, but from Jewish values and Jewish ethics.

Bennett wears many lay leadership hats. At the time of our interview, she was serving on the executive committee of the U.S. Holocaust Memorial Museum and the AJCommittee, chairing Project Interchange (which brings non-Jewish "influentials" to Israel), co-chairing a capital campaign for the Gesher Jewish Day School, and serving on the board of the endowment fund for the Jewish Federation of Greater Washington. And that is a partial list of her communal duties. "I've got to do things because other people don't ... who don't feel the compulsion or compassion for the Jewish community," said Bennett, who is involved in philanthropy as well as organizational governance.

Her earlier experience as an inactive, unaffiliated Jew directs her path today, she says. "I am a believer in an incredibly big Abrahamic tent," Bennett said. "I want that tent to have enough doors, or flaps, to allow people to come in, as long as they feel a part of the Jewish people. It is absolutely what drives me in everything I do."

A Route to Learning

Communal callings also draw people who long to learn more about the Jewish tradition. In my own case, close to a decade writing for the Jewish press and communal field strengthened my grasp of Judaic history and religion. That gift of knowledge lent meaning to even the most frenzied deadlines and mundane assignments. In a parallel way, taking a job in the development department of her local Jewish federation was an education in Judaism for Cathy Winick. "Before I worked here, I didn't know Pesach and Passover were the same thing," admitted Winick, who grew up with a strong dose of Jewish culture but minimal religion. She describes her entry into the Jewish communal world, several months after her father's death, as a stroke of destiny, a milestone on her Jewish journey. "There was no accident or mistake; it wasn't that I was looking for work," Winick said. "This was *bashert* [destiny]."

It was the challenge of sharing the Jewish knowledge that she herself was learning with other families that propelled Joanne Doades onto her path as a Jewish educator and author. Now charged with curriculum development for lifelong learning in the Reform movement, Doades began by launching a Shabbat group for families of young children at New York's Central Synagogue in the late 1980s. That led her into other work as a Judaic specialist with a Jewish nursery school, and later, as a director of Jewish programs for the Educational Alliance (now the city's Fourteenth Street Y), doing outreach and parent education, often with unaffiliated Jews—like she once was.

"The writing of curriculum was following what was happening in my own life," recalled Doades, who by then was the mother of three and holding Shabbat dinners at home as an early step toward Jewish observance. Supporting other Jews to deepen their learning, as she once was guided in turn, now fills her workdays. "It's a life filled with purpose and meaning," Doades said. "It's a belief that there's a system of behavior that matters and an awareness of the fact that we strengthen one another and help one another grow to be even better than we were yesterday."

Models of Service

To even picture a career of communal engagement often takes knowing someone who walks in those shoes and makes the effort seem worth undertaking. And an encounter with another's deep commitment to the path of service can reverberate for years. As a high school student, years before his path led him to rabbinical school, Ethan Seidel pondered converting to Quakerism. When his parents got wind of his plans, they convinced him to see the man who had married them, the late

Rabbi Jacob Kraft, of Wilmington, Delaware. Seidel still can recall sitting in the rabbi's study decades ago, and scanning the bookshelves bursting with volumes Seidel had yet to open. One searching question from the older man still reverberates from their meeting. "Do you have any sense of what you're leaving?" Seidel recalls Kraft asking him, gesturing toward the books that lined his study.

The rabbi had intuited the spiritual and intellectual thirst of the alienated college-bound youth in front of him. And that single question was enough to pique young Seidel's interest about the rest of what he had missed. "I wasn't leaving Judaism just to rebel," Seidel said. "I was looking for some serious religious experience, and it hadn't occurred to me that what I was exposed to—expensive bar mitzvahs—wasn't all there was."

Later, at the Oberlin College campus, Seidel began spending time at the "kosher co-op," where he would find another mentor, Hillel Rabbi Shimon Brandt. Though Brandt was Orthodox and Seidel grew up Conservative, the younger man discovered in this rabbi a person to whom he could bring his questions. Their intellectual jousting helped Seidel feel at ease again in Jewish life. Said Seidel of Brandt, "It was like finding a tennis partner, who is as good as you are or better."

Kraft, the rabbi who helped set Seidel on the road home to Judaism, has been gone for nearly two decades now, but the younger man can recite by heart the words on his tombstone: *Ohev et-habriot um-karvan laTorah* ("Loving fellow creatures and drawing them near to Torah"). "That's my goal as a rabbi: to do for others what he did for me," Seidel said. "It's that openness to helping people when they're ready for the next step that's at the core of my mission."

Reframing Communal Roles

And among at least part of the next generation of Jewish communal leaders, one finds future rabbis and cantors with an original vision of their roles, limned by the circuitous paths they have taken on their own spiritual quests.

Nondenominational rabbinical student Margie Klein found her calling while being arrested with two dozen clergy, mostly Christian priests and ministers, as they conducted a sit-in in solidarity with nursing-home workers. She remembers the impact made by the people of the cloth when they came to a later court hearing in religious garb. "The religious community had a kind of truth and a kind of courage that I wanted to find," she recalled. Some years would go by—filled with social and political activism—before Klein, now a nondenominational rabbinic student, would pursue that dream. "I've had this feeling repeatedly in my life that I have a calling," Klein explained. "I don't believe angels are flying around us, but I do believe that sometimes people speak the voice of God or allow us to hear it and allow us to understand more deeply who we are or who we're supposed to be." From activist clergy and from civil rights movement veterans with a deep vein of faith, Klein heard the call to become a spiritual leader in her own Jewish tradition, with justice on her mind.

For his part, professional musician turned cantorial student Randy Herman has a flip answer and a serious one about the vocation he has chosen. He was bequeathed a pair of contrasting legacies from his paternal grandparents who performed in vaudeville, on the one hand, and his religiously devout maternal grandparents on the other. "You put the Orthodox and vaudevillian grandparents together and you get a performing cantor," Herman quipped.

In a more earnest vein, Herman points out the distinct roles he plays as a musician on the concert stage and as a cantorial soloist on the *bimah*. His new calling as a cantor has drawn him outside the boundaries of the performer's ego. The people listening to him in shul "are not there applauding; they're here to be inspired and have their own experience,"

Herman said. "You're modeling, being engaged with, and having a musical conversation with the divine mystery."

Jewish seekers once disenchanted from their faith, like those profiled in this chapter, have special gifts to offer as communal leaders. They can provide insight into what drives people away from Judaism and what brings them back. They are more apt to remember that an atmosphere of warmth and a context of meaning that illumines individual lives and social issues of the day build loyalty to Jewish institutions far deeper than any dues structure. These Jews who have returned know that those on the road home to Judaism face obstacles, setbacks, and their own fears, but encouraging words from a kindred spirit can speed the way.

13 Pathless in the Promised Land

Blazing Jewish Trails

S tand, legs spread wide and firmly planted, with your left foot tilting slightly inward and the other foot at a right angle. Raise your arms to shoulder height, then bend to the right until your arms are perpendicular to the ground, with the lower hand stretching earthward, the upper hand reaching for the sky. That's the classic Triangle Pose of hatha yoga—an apt expression of the Jewish value of *hishtavut*, equanimity or balance, says Rabbi Myriam Klotz. In a physical sense, we achieve that equilibrium "by reaching up and grounding down at the same time," said Klotz, who co-directs the integration of yoga and Judaism at New York's Institute for Jewish Spirituality.

This fusion of East and West represents just one of several new frontiers in Judaism, areas where innovators are adapting disciplines or causes not always thought of as Jewish to further spiritual growth and strengthen religious identity. As taught by Klotz and others, Jewish yoga combines the ancient poses of hatha yoga with such theological ideas as *hishtavut*, with Hebrew letters, or with prayers.

Another area of fresh terrain in Judaism is spiritual direction, in which seekers meet with a single advisor or with a group of like-minded people to map their inward journey and set goals for spiritual growth. In a different way, many activist Jews are finding a portal into Jewish life through faith-based environmental groups and programs. Though much more recent in its origins than the broader social justice tradition in Judaism, the Jewish green movement is persuading new constituencies to reconsider Judaism on the strength of its teachings about stewardship of the Earth's resources and the living world.

There will be some within the religious establishment who view these newer pathways—Jewish yoga, spiritual direction, and environmentalism—as not Jewish enough. Yet, though these pursuits may not speak to a majority of Jews, they are meeting the needs of some who cannot or will not walk through other doors into the Jewish community. Those in search of a less cerebral entree to Judaism than traditional text study may find the ideas behind those texts reinvigorated by Jewish yoga. Other Jews in or out of congregations who are seeking a contemplative road to spirituality will find in spiritual direction a useful tool. And activists fired by the global conversation on climate change, biodiversity, and other environmental concerns may be thrilled to learn how much Judaism has to say about the values they hold dear.

Meanwhile, it is worth noting that the Jewish tradition of borrowing practices from the surrounding culture goes back hundreds of years. Jews have often adapted the languages, foods, folkways, and intellectual heritage of the many lands where they have settled. What we now think of as Jewish liturgical music, for instance, carries echoes of European classical music, Eastern European folk tunes, and, most recently,

American popular songs. Such borrowings have enriched Judaism.

Today, say advocates of Jewish yoga, increasing numbers of Jews want to grasp the wisdom of their tradition through their muscles as well as their minds. "More and more of us are coming to Torah with body-based eyes," said Klotz. "Every Torah portion, every verse, can be viewed through a kinesthetic lens in the same way that a feminist lens is a powerful way to view Torah." Books such as *Torah Yoga* by Diane Bloomfield and *Aleph-Bet Yoga: Embodying the Hebrew Letters for Physical and Spiritual Well-Being* (Jewish Lights) by Steven A. Rapp document the recent blending of yoga's physical discipline with Judaism's intellectual and mystical heritage.

Following Green Pathways

The Jewish environmental movement—as can be seen at any gathering of the Coalition on the Environment and Jewish Life or many local Jewish green groups around the country—is luring younger Jews who might not otherwise feel the tug of personal relevance in the congregations where many grew up. Jeremy Manela, twenty-five, personifies this phenomenon. At the Pearlstone Conference and Retreat Center in Reisterstown, Maryland, he works as farm director, raising organic produce for Baltimore's Jewish community. Days before my interview with him, Manela had celebrated his wedding to another green activist, Kaylin (who goes by her Hebrew name, Netsitsa), in a ceremony replete with such traditional customs as a *tish* (table) for the bride and groom, where friends could greet them individually, and a *bedecken* (veiling) of the bride at the wedding ceremony. "I try to learn what the traditions are," said Manela, who practices tai chi with his eclectic Judaism. He had previously taught at the Teva Learning Center, which offers Jewish environmental education to Jewish day schools and adults across the denominations.

Raised in Potomac, Maryland, an affluent suburb of Washington, D.C., Manela developed a sense of "awe" and soulful "immersion" in a grander world of nature on family camping trips in the Shenandoah Mountains and oceanside vacations. Religious education did not pluck the same spiritual chords, said Manela, who admits loathing Hebrew school. Yet, as he grew up, hearing about the experience of his paternal grandparents, who were Holocaust survivors, lent him a sense of inner strength, a realization "that my people and my family had been through the fire. Just witnessing to their story and to the horrific aspects of humanity may have spurred my *tikkun olam* work," Manela said. But for years, he was unsure how and where to direct his own energies.

A trip to Israel at seventeen got him reading Torah in a way Hebrew school and synagogue had not. Suddenly, he was finding in Judaism "an endless ocean of thought, ethics, philosophy, culture." People in Israel, even amid economic and security challenges, seemed to possess an inner poise, even joy, that, for the visiting teen, trumped the material plenty of the Washington suburbs he knew. "Despite the fact that Israelis don't have many things that Americans have, they have a certain toughness, strength, and contentment we don't have," Manela observed, noting that his visit to the Jewish state eight years ago was his "first real immersion in a world with a different compass." Meanwhile, a visit to an Israeli kibbutz planted the seeds for his life on the land in Maryland and prompted him to take an agronomy class along with Jewish, Hebrew, and global environmental studies at the University of Wisconsin.

As he tills the soil in Reisterstown today, he is cultivating his own crop of Jewish values, hybrids of new and old. "I'm trying to create a culture of intention and quality in relationships, connections—myself and the earth, myself and others, myself and God," Manela said. "Investing in the relationship with the Earth and other people fills my spirit and brings more light into my life."

The birth of a daughter brought another Jew into congregational life, but her Reform temple's environmental focus kept her there. Dian Seidel, forty-eight, is a research scientist in climate change. On the side, she serves on the Green Shalom committee at Temple Emanuel in Kensington, Maryland. "If we were childless, I'm not sure we'd be part of a synagogue, but I'm glad we are," said the Chevy Chase, Maryland, woman. "There is a power behind the environmental perspective coming from a religious base."

A longtime champion of environmental causes, Rabbi Fred Scherlinder Dobb has met many people like Seidel and Manela, who have found green niches in Jewish life. Indeed, he suggests, some might not join the religious community otherwise. Dobb has heard that message from members of his own Adat Shalom Reconstructionist Congregation in Bethesda, Maryland, which built a synagogue based on green building principles in 2001. Looking back to the early years of Jewish green activism, Dobb flags his 1990 cross-country trek with the Global Walk for a Liveable World, in which he served as an unofficial Jewish spokesperson. During the first of hundreds of talks to Jewish communities en route, he recalled a student who came up to him at the Hillel center at the University of California, Santa Barbara. She had not set foot in shul since her bat mitzvah, but she *had* chaired the campus recycling club, and Dobb's remarks stirred her. "'I don't want to make a big deal, but this kind of gave me a reason to stay Jewish,'" Dobb remembered her saying. "It was not my eloquence that sealed the deal, but simply the exposure to what too few people understand even today: Jewish tradition is unbelievably forward thinking when it comes to creation care."

Close to two decades later, "creation care" is shorthand for a new awareness of the environment across the Jewish world.

Green-leaning institutions such as Teva; Adamah: The Jewish Environmental Fellowship; Hazon, which promotes Jewish engagement through outdoor and environmental education; the Coalition on the Environment and Jewish Life; and grass-roots green groups around the country are funneling Jews into synagogues. And as environmental activists join congregations, argues Dobb, these new members gain the sustenance of spiritual values and camaraderie that can sustain them in hard times. Judaism "grounds its adherents in something sacred and time-tested, which helps them stay in it for the long haul," Dobb said. "It's also not just a tradition; it's a community."

Guidance on the Journey

For Jews who prefer to contemplate, the emerging field of spiritual direction has much to offer. Many seekers need not only a place to discuss their inner life, but also some guidance navigating the dense brush of Jewish teachings. New York Jewish educator Linda Thal co-directs the Yedidya Center for Spiritual Direction, which trains rabbis in spiritual direction. She is also writing a curriculum on adult spirituality for the Institute for Jewish Spirituality. In her own practice, she has most contact with Jews who belong to congregations but seek "spiritual deepening." Yet she also sees the potential to reach others at the margins.

Spiritual direction, she said, quenches a thirst for a relationship with God—one often prayed for, but rarely discussed in the Jewish community. It can help people unify the disparate pathways of Jewish tradition. Spiritual direction is also a magnet for those who are eager to chart their Jewish course in the company of kindred spirits. "Some of it is about the loneliness of the spiritual journey and not having companions, conversational partners, or support," Thal said. A spiritual director for eight years, Ann Kline notices some patterns in the twenty-two Jewish clients with whom she has worked. Calling them "God wrestlers," she sees them both embracing and struggling with their religious heritage. All have affiliated outside the major denominations, in the more experimental corners of the Jewish world: Reconstructionism, Jewish Renewal, *chavurah*, or Jewish humanism. "They're people who want a very personal engagement with God and the tradition, and they have not been able to find that kind of personal engagement in mainstream Reform and Conservative congregations," Kline said.

One roadblock on their journey, she believes, is something that this former lawyer calls the "Jewish exclusivity clause." In her conversations with clients, Kline hears a frustration that mainstream "Judaism is about being Jewish, but it's not about the bigger world, and we live in the bigger world. That's not what I hear in the Buddhist community: it's about how to be a compassionate human being in the world, not about identifying strongly as Buddhist." Meeting the religious needs of her clients has meant offering them such practical options as group spiritual direction and such spiritual tools as meditation, reflection, and retreat. These tools, Kline contends, "are not antithetical to Jewish life, but can enrich Jewish life and, in fact, are practices that have been used in Jewish communities for centuries."

During a decade of doing spiritual direction for herself as well, Kline says she's found her own song in the larger chorus of mainstream Judaism. In this intimate process, "I'm encouraged to claim my own voice, and to reflect on my experience of God and how I live in relation to that," Kline said, citing the "unconditional acceptance" she finds in talks with her advisor. Kline's qualms about the Jewish establishment have not disappeared, but having a channel for them has helped immeasurably, she says. "I still have the questions and challenges, but having a place where I can express them safely makes it possible for me to remain in Jewish life," Kline said. "Without it, I don't know that I would be able to maintain that."

Testing New Paradigms

The new pathways into Jewish life have arisen, in part, through the efforts of people who felt like outsiders within the old paradigms. Take the case of yoga advocate Klotz, who, for five or six years, shelved her religious heritage. Preoccupied by her emerging lesbian identity in college, she noted, "I did everything but study Judaism." Yet she chose a junior year abroad in Israel and returned to major in religious studies at Brown University. The rabbinate appealed to her growing spiritual thirst, but she did not wish to be in the closet at the Jewish Theological Seminary, the Conservative movement's seminary, which at that time did not ordain gays and lesbians. Torn, Klotz moved to California and dropped out of Jewish life as she explored paganism and sought wisdom in feminism, yoga, and holistic healing. During this period, she earned a master's degree in photography and creative writing, trained to become a yoga teacher, and studied massage and yoga therapies. In those other fields, "nobody was telling me to deny my body and my body's truth in order to be with God," Klotz said.

A conversation with Rabbi Michael Lerner about her new interests first gave Klotz the idea of combining them with Jewish practice. "'One day, you'll bring that back to Judaism,'" she recalled him saying. "He was sort of a *moreh derech* [spiritual advisor] for me at that moment." A short time later, she took a job teaching Hebrew to children and applied to the Reconstructionist Rabbinical College, where she worked her way through the program, supporting herself through her yoga and massage skills.

Some may argue that Jewish yoga and other newer spiritual pursuits risk turning Jews too far inward and away from the communal orientation of Judaism. Addressing that concern, Thal said, "If it's authentic spirituality, it should be stripping away the self-centeredness, the narcissism, the self-concern." For Jews, a useful spiritual direction, she says, will concentrate on practicing *mitzvot* and building community. "It's not a religion that focuses on the individual," Thal said. "You can't do it alone."

Will exploring spiritual direction, protecting the environment, and adapting yoga to Jewish principles fire the imagination of tomorrow's seekers? Will the online outpourings on Jewish blogs and the ecstatic rhythms of Jewish drumming circles, to name a couple of other emerging practices, become lasting features of Jewish life? Like all borrowings from the larger culture, some of today's innovations may not survive the initial enthusiasms that fueled them. Others will endure to feed the souls of future Jewish generations.

14 Valley of the Shadow
Healing Body and Soul

Terry Spodick can remember the instant she began to take Judaism to heart. At forty, in the wake of a diagnosis of terminal lymphoma, she took her seat in a cancer support group. Next to her sat Sally, a sixtyish woman wearing a wig and conservative clothes, who was coping with a similar death sentence. Asked by a guest speaker to say what gave them strength, Spodick heard her neighbor, who would live another eight years, answer: "My faith." The authority behind those two words moved the Jewish woman listening to reappraise her own spiritual life. "It was the inner strength and power that woman had—you could almost touch it," Spodick recalled. "I really felt all the walls I had put up to nearly all forms of organized religion came crashing down. That was the moment that just opened the door."

Catalysts for Growth

In times of stress, loss, illness, and the specter of death, some Jews experience doors opening to a force greater than themselves. No one would willingly pursue that kind of suffering for its occasional spiritual gifts. And yet such unsought experiences, in ways unpredictable and often inexplicable, can propel people forward on the road of spiritual growth.

Decades ago, Philip Mandelkorn watched his dreams of a better world splinter beyond recognition. He recalls covering the civil rights beat for *Time* magazine when civil rights leader Martin Luther King, Jr. was slain in April 1968. Then, in June of the same year, the journalist-turned-speechwriter for Robert F. Kennedy was close to another tragedy, as the Democratic presidential contender was gunned down in a Los Angeles hotel. "I was catapulted into my spiritual journey," Mandelkorn said of the assassinations of King and Kennedy. "When they disappeared from the planet, I lost my sense of hope for the country."

He quit the world of politics and took off for what he thought would be a trek to India and Nepal. But a stopover in Israel became a stay of several months. He picked tangerines on a kibbutz, dropped in on former Prime Minister David Ben-Gurion, and toured holy sites. "Every place I went, my heart was tapped," Mandelkorn said, recalling visits to such places as Rachel's Tomb and the Mosque of Omar. "After the experiences of the late sixties, with these great people getting killed almost before my eyes, I had a wounded heart, an open heart."

He would go to Jerusalem's Western Wall and weep, then marvel at his own response. A Navy veteran, Mandelkorn hailed from a military family and was not at ease with strong emotion. "You're a tough Seal, a Navy frogman," he told himself. "You don't cry." The ancient stones of the Western Wall were speaking to him in a language he had yet to translate. "As my guru told me, when you make a pilgrimage to a holy place, it plants seeds in you that sprout later," Mandelkorn said.

In a kind of daze, he wandered from Israel to Mexico for a year, where he experimented with psychedelic drugs and dabbled in Sufism, and then on to New York City. Yet the interest in his Jewish roots stirred up by his trip to Israel kept surfacing. During this period, he had a vision of King David and felt a deep kinship with this figure of Jewish antiquity. Another time, he found a sense of religious identity etched in his own bearded face. "I looked into a mirror once in Mexico and saw a young Hasid looking at me," Mandelkorn said.

An article on LSD by Rabbi Zalman Schachter (now Schachter-Shalomi) prompted him to write a letter to the scholar and Jewish Renewal leader. Their correspondence over some years eventually led Mandelkorn to join Schachter in Winnipeg, Canada, where they collaborated on a book about Jewish mysticism, *Fragments of a Future Scroll: Hassidism for the Aquarian Age*. The year after he wrote to the rabbi, Mandelkorn also made contact with Swami Satchinanda, the yoga master who would become his guru. For Mandelkorn, both Judaism and yoga have served as a "set of walking sticks for spiritual awakening and enlightenment." And, it would seem, healing in the aftermath of emotional trauma.

Fixing Frayed Relationships

For many people, meanwhile, emotional wounds are more likely to come from family strife than from the winds of history. In such cases, Rabbi Leila Gal Berner has found Jewish ideas about forgiveness have moved her from hurt to healing. Just above the computer monitor in Berner's home office hang eleven words from antiquity. "Be kind, for everyone you meet is fighting a great battle," reads the banner, a quote from first-century Jewish philosopher Philo of Alexandria.

Teachings like Philo's—along with the Jewish imperative of *shalom bayit* (peace in the home)—have informed Berner's efforts to heal troubled family relationships. As she has sought to live these values, Berner has reached some personal conclusions that diverge from pop psychology. That has meant, she said, "realizing that some things are better left to be let go of, even if they're unresolved." Making peace with another person matters most. In Berner's view of interpersonal tangles, the Jewish mandate to treat others as we would wish to be treated trumps the natural desire for self-expression and closure on the traumas of one's past. "The greater imperative is *'V'ahavta l're'eycha kamocha,'* 'love your fellow human being as yourself,'" Berner said. "Nothing is worth violating that, ultimately."

Healing of an acute physical kind has also been a part of Berner's journey. Her now teenaged daughter, Kayla, was born with a heart anomaly that required surgical intervention when she was just three months old. Some twenty to thirty rabbinic colleagues gathered at the hospital to lend support. For an instant, she had a vision of hands holding Kayla's heart. She turned to her partner and said, "She's going to be okay." Berner stresses that she sees her daughter's healing as more natural than supernatural, yet for her, it has a spiritual dimension. "As a Reconstructionist, I don't actually believe in miracles," she explained, "but I do believe in a sacred process where all the pieces are working together—the doctors, the nurses, Kayla's own spirit, and community support."

Illness as a Teacher

Illness did not launch Rayzl Feuer's religious quest, but the experience became a significant part of her journey. Battling breast cancer, she found support in the *Mi Shebeirach* prayer for healing chanted in her name by her congregation during her year of medical treatment. "I already believed in the power of prayer," Feuer said. "It meant a lot to me." In service to other cancer patients, meanwhile, she found a deep sense of purpose. She volunteered as an assistant to others struggling with cancer, fixing their hair, offering massage, and helping one dying woman make an audiotape for her baby daughter.

"Our encounter was an extraordinary gift to both of us," Feuer said. "We were each other's angel."

Like others interviewed, she seized the opportunity to grow amid the suffering of ill health and emerged with a spiritual strength she had not possessed before. "God has been molding me as one molds steel," Feuer said. "Steel is molded, toughened, and churned to make it strong." Whatever the days bring, she says she holds fast to two Jewish rituals: the *Modah Ani* prayer upon arising and the bedtime *Shema*. "When I go to sleep at night, I'm acknowledging I might not get up," explained this cancer survivor. "When I get up in the morning, I want to see it as a gift."

For Rabbi Hava Pell, Judaism was a critical part of her toolbox of healing from compulsive eating. At the time, she admits, food had become a form of idolatry for her: "my comfort, my best friend, and my god." Taking herself off this self-destructive path took attending a residential treatment program for food addiction and, for some three years, daily support-group meetings. These early moves toward healing gave Pell a fresh perspective on Jewish teachings. "I found I could go back to the prayer book and it was all there; God is all goodness and all connection; God restores my soul; God offers justice and balance, which I was desperately seeking, inner peace, serenity, and wholeness," Pell said. In her evolving understanding of faith, inner healing does not guarantee specific outcomes for body and mind. "God promises to be a soul guard—not a body guard," Pell said. "Our souls can always be held and comforted no matter how our bodies are buffeted."

For rabbinical student Debra Kolodny, meanwhile, the Hebrew psalms have had a power to knit her together when she feels inwardly torn. "When I've gone through emotional trauma, drama, *tehilim*, or psalms, come through me and keep me together," Kolodny said. She sang psalms at the hospital bedside of her sedated father, as he recovered from the near-fatal effects of surgery. Nonresponsive at the start, her secular father evinced a noticeable physical reaction when she began her chanting, Kolodny remembers. "When I started singing, he lifted up his neck and turned his head toward my voice," Kolodny said. In the course of three hours, she recalls watching his vital signs strengthen on the hospital monitors nearby. "I saw his heart rate stabilize and his oxygen stabilize and his fever go away," Kolodny reported. Her father recuperated fully, aside from prior heart damage. "I believe one hundred percent that the psalms healed him," Kolodny said.

Was it the healing power of music, the sonorities of a beloved voice, the sounds of the Hebrew words, or a moment of divine embrace? The people profiled in this book would not be of one mind, but for many, following a spiritual path in Judaism has undeniably brought a renewed sense of shalom, in the sense of both peace and well-being or wholeness.

The Lessons of Loss

That kind of healing comes hard in the aftermath of personal loss, especially the death of a parent or a mate. Even after grievous illness, the body's organs and tissues often knit together far quicker than a devastated spirit. In her work as a chaplain, Jewish Renewal rabbi Tsurah August has drawn on her path of healing from the early loss of her father. "My own life experience has been working from brokenness to wholeness," August said.

She sees that human journey as a theme underlying much of Jewish practice. "Judaism is about wholeness, oneness, completeness—from the rituals to the construct of community to the melodies and singing," August said. "Judaism creates a vessel for every time of our life, and there are those resources for meaning, comfort, and connection, no matter what we're going through." As one practical example, she cites the tradition of the *shivah*, the open house held by a mourning family in the week after a death. In this setting, members of the Jewish community have the duty to comfort the mourners and, she points out, the mourners are obliged to accept that support. "It is a beautifully balanced reciprocity," August said.

An experience of personal loss set Norma Brooks on a journey of spiritual discovery, with musical accompaniment. A scan of her early biography does not foreshadow a future composer of liturgical melodies or the cofounder of Shalshalet, an organization dedicated to showcasing new settings of Jewish liturgy. "I had no idea Hebrew was associated in any way with being Jewish," recalled Brooks of her Brooklyn girlhood attending Yiddish *shule*. Her mother instilled in her daughter a secular outlook, forbidding her even to wear a Jewish star.

Yet decades later, Brooks found a new vocation rooted in Judaism a year after the untimely death in 1983 of her husband, Paul Lichterman. For her, Lichterman had been not only a life companion but also a guide on her religious path in Judaism. As the first *yahrzeit* (anniversary) of Lichterman's passing neared, Brooks turned to her musical talents to keep his spirit alive. The result, *"Ul'amtuye,"* was no dirge, but a melody that nearly bounced with joy, reflecting the hopeful message of the text, a prayer used before public Torah readings from the Zohar, a book of Jewish mystical thought: *"Ul'amtuye lana mi tuv nehorakh/ul'kabel tz'lotana b'rahamin"* ("And may You bestow on us of Your bountiful light / and receive our prayer in compassion"). "The composing was always connected to spirit, transcendence," Brooks said. "It was the only door I could open after Paul died."

"Ul'amtuye" would become the first of many such compositions penned over more than two decades, collected in *Your Bountiful Light: New Music for Jewish Liturgy* (a book and CD), compositions most connected to a person in Brooks' circle and a life-cycle event—from a bar mitzvah to an anniversary to a posthumous tribute. "It is my spiritual anchor," Brooks said.

"The music and composing gave me a total comfort level with prayer."

A Spiritual Opening

Meanwhile, against overwhelming odds, Spodick weathered her lymphoma and sixteen years later, reports a full life. She credits the love and support of family and friends, along with her medical treatment, as key factors in her recovery. Ed, a friend and fellow entrepreneur, served as a sounding board as she weighed the advice of doctors and Jewish ethics in planning her chemotherapy, which she first sought to halt when she reacted adversely to one of the drugs.

The spiritual opening occasioned by treading at the gates of death, in the company of some religious role models, altered her forever. "Sometimes it is that we're truly given the gift to deal with problems we have and sometimes that gift is faith or religion," said Spodick. Ed became a Jewish mentor as Spodick began exploring the Judaism she had kept at a safe distance throughout most of her life. "My respect and affection for someone who was a devout, practicing Jew opened up doors," she said.

The aftereffects of chemotherapy left Spodick muddled. To sharpen her mind, she set herself the task of learning Hebrew. That effort, in turn, prompted her to join an adult bat mitzvah class at the temple she had barely attended before. "My sense was I was going to suffer, but I was going to survive," Spodick said. "At that point, I just made a conscious decision that I wasn't going to worry about dying and I was going to put my trust in God or a higher being."

Spodick would go on to plunge into Jewish life, becoming a board member of her congregation, Temple Beth El and Jewish Community Center in Apto, California, and caring for a local Jewish cemetery. She also helped create a tool to support others confronting an illness like hers. With the co-leader of her cancer support group, Julie Martin-Pitts, she wrote the self-published *Diagnosis Cancer: What Do I Do Now?* "This path I believe has given me the opportunity to be a better person," Spodick said.

Life's wounds, whether of personal loss, grievous injury, or serious illness, create a certain vulnerability. At those times, the rarified state that sometimes accompanies physical or emotional fragility can prompt a contemplative mood. I experienced that kind of a spiritual opening while laid low by illness some dozen years ago. Too weak to do much more than rest, I felt a keen joy in watching squirrels frolic in a poplar tree outside my apartment window. When disease sapped my strength, and an uncertain diagnosis left me torn between hope and despair, I learned, in a way I can sometimes still remember, to find blessing in small things.

To seek reason for gratitude in the midst of loss and illness is not to minimize the anguish of such experiences. When the body is weak, the spirits are low, and demands of daily life seem overwhelming, giving thanks does not come easy. Yet, Judaism calls us to count our blessings, even in the details of well-being, from waking up in the morning (acknowledged in the *Modeh Ani*) to having internal plumbing that works (noted in the *Asher Yatzar* prayer). References to hope and healing triumphing over hardship abound in the poetry of the Psalms. In one of the most famous, Psalm 23, the speaker moves in just a few lines from the "valley of the shadow of death" to the expectation of "goodness and love" and a long life ahead. "The Lord is my shepherd," reads the opening line, suggesting that even in life's bleakest moments, the opportunity remains to "dwell in the house of the Lord," however we may define that experience.

III

Dwelling
Places

15 The Burning Bush
Glimpses of the Divine

Maggie Anton used to sleepwalk, spiritually speaking, through Yom Kippur, the Jewish Day of Atonement, without a genuine grasp of the day's significance. What's more, the appeals for God's mercy and compassion that laced the holiday liturgy rang hollow for the California biochemist, as they did for other Jews she knew. "I was relieved it was perfectly normal to be a Jewish agnostic," Anton said of her state of belief at the time.

Her religious awareness moved to a new level one afternoon at her neighborhood gym. Anton was toning her abdominal muscles on Shabbat Shuva, the sabbath that falls between Rosh Hashanah and Yom Kippur, when a presence took her by surprise. "All of a sudden, I felt I wasn't alone in the gym and got a feeling of love and disappointment," Anton recalled. "Believe me, if I hadn't been lying down, I would have fallen down. I was doing sit-ups, and God spoke to me."

Only a small fraction of the people profiled in these pages describe a direct encounter with the Divine. Even their understanding of divinity varies wildly. Some deeply believe in a personal God who intervenes in history and individual lives. Others favor a more Reconstructionist model, a synergy of human efforts that, at their best, can heal the body, mend the soul, and better the world. Yet others remain the Jewish agnostics that Anton once was. Still another group claims the mantle of atheism, while contributing to Jewish communal life and following many of the *mitzvot* of Judaism.

Yet, for the few who report coming close to God, the experience seems to be life-altering, often transforming a purely rationalist outlook into one that melds worldly knowledge with the wisdom of faith. Anton said she knew at once the reason for her own visitation. Gnawing at her conscience was the memory of stepping over an ethical line, switching tags on clothes she purchased at a discount store. Struck dumb in her gym clothes, she believed she was being asked to halt a practice that violated the moral code she was learning in her studies of Talmud.

Bridging Two Worlds

Many Jews who have excelled in their secular educations and amassed advanced degrees, but feel like beginners in their spiritual lives, find joy in cultivating a new sense of the Divine.

Environmental consultant Jonathan Rosenfield is also developing his own eclectic notion of God. "There are important things to understand about life that aren't just cerebral, that you're not going to get from a double-blind study," said Rosenfield. He points to a stumbling block to a comfortable relationship with the Divine for many committed to egalitarian ideals: the imagery of kingship. In traditional Jewish blessings and prayers, God is addressed as *Melech ha'olam* (literally, "King," but often translated as Sovereign of the universe).

Many feminists object to the gendered view of God and the imagery of dominance implicit in the word, *Melech*.

Rosenfield appreciates those concerns, but he also finds a powerful subtext in the traditional God language. "As a white man with advanced degrees in today's society, part of what I get from religion is a reminder to be humble," he said. "I can also understand why women and other groups in our society would not need that language."

Others in the liberal streams of Judaism find themselves ill at ease with a king-subject model of human engagement with the Divine. From the writers of Reconstructionist *siddurim* to poet-liturgist Marcia Falk, contemporary Jews have wrestled with, and sometimes transformed, the language and object of prayer. In some new formulations, *Melech ha'olam* has morphed into the gender-neutral, transpersonal *Ruach ha'olam* (Spirit of the universe).

As for Rosenfield, he finds the makings of a divine model he can live with in the biblical stories (Genesis 18) of Abraham and the three strangers, and the Jewish patriarch's arguments with God over the fate of Sodom and Gomorrah. "This is a force you can plead with, reprimand, argue with," Rosenfield said. "There's king language but it doesn't mean you're a complete servant. You're in relationship." A Jewish faith in God, he believes, implies a mandate to act according to a moral code with regard to the treatment of others. "You have to run out and greet strangers and plead with God, with the universe, when you think the universe is unjust," Rosenfield said.

As he grows in his own understanding, the Berkeley, California, man sees a convergence of what he knows in two parallel disciplines, Judaism and biology. "What's fascinating to me is that we walk around today thinking science and religion have nothing to do with each other—or that they're in competition," said Rosenfield. "Here are two ways of studying reality and they speak in different languages." He has come to apply what he sees as a lesson from the creation story of Genesis to his own work. In the biblical telling, God not only fashions the natural world, but also contemplates it afterward, declaring it *"tov"* ("good"). Of his own earthly endeavors, Rosenfield said, "If I create something, it's not done when it's done, but when I've reflected on it." As in the Genesis narrative, it also matters "to see that it's good." A habit of scientific speculation helped Rosenfield make Jewish teachings his own.

Dancing toward the Divine

For another Jewish thinker, meanwhile, the creative process led to a new experience of God. With a literal wave of her arms, Tsurah August began reclaiming her Jewish soul. In her mid-twenties, the New York dancer got a choreography assignment that transformed her spiritual self-image. At a master class with Israeli-American choreographer Anna Sokolow, August was asked to create a dance about her roots. She found herself re-creating the traditional gesture of making circles over Shabbat candles. "That movement," she recalled, "brought me back." Her dance piece, "Family Ties," incorporated that circling motion—even though she'd never done it as a child. As August explored her Jewish identity in movement, Sokolow urged her on, becoming a creative mentor.

Through her experiments in choreography, August started to integrate the disparate strands of her life. "I began putting my spirituality, dance, and Judaism together—to have them become one and to understand they were one; these were deep expressions of my Jewish soul," she said. "From that, I moved into the rest of Judaism." Even today, as a rabbi and hospice chaplain, creative movement continues to inform her understanding of Judaism and the Divine. "My paradigm of God is interconnectedness and interrelatedness ... and I experience that through dance," August said.

Visits to one of Judaism's holy sites have sparked the spiritual choreography of other Jews. Debra Kolodny once believed only in causes. Her sense of a force greater than herself emerged at sixteen when she took a trip to Israel, amid worries about her brother, who was in the hospital at the time. On a visit to the Kotel, or Western Wall, she had an encounter with a presence she could not rationally explain. "I had an experience that I was sure then and am sure now was God," said Kolodny. Then a secular Jew, she wasn't sure how to pray. Yet, she stuck a note that asked for her brother's healing into a cranny of the ancient stones and stood there for a time. "The air got thick and I felt engulfed by a sentient presence," recalled the Maryland woman, who came home a few weeks later to find her brother recovered. As for herself, the experience lingered in a sustained sense of the Divine. "I became a small *kuf* Kabbalist," said Kolodny, using the Hebrew letter that starts the word *Kabbalah*, a word that describes the realm of Jewish mysticism. In that moment at the Kotel, that esoteric realm became real for Kolodny.

Words for the Ineffable

Defining God becomes a struggle for some returning Jews. Richard Chused hews to traditional Jewish practice, observing Shabbat and keeping kosher, but takes issue with the images of divine omnipotence found in Torah. "For a lot of contemporary Jews, it's impossible to deal with a *deus ex machina* God," Chused said. "It doesn't fit modern sensibilities." Yet this law professor and Conservative Jew finds meaning in a more modern notion of God, who may not step in as a universal fixer, yet can lift people above mundane concerns. His working definition reminds him to look beyond his own set of personal concerns. "There's something more important than you out there," Chused said. "It forces you to step back and pay less attention to yourself and more to other people, and to community."

Jewish Renewal teachers helped Judith Dack reframe her notion of God in a way that finally made sense to her. A decade ago, rabbinic pastor Andy Gold gave Dack an interpretation that dispelled her religious alienation. On a retreat at Rose Mountain in New Mexico, they stopped at a lookout with a spectacular view. "'God is not an old man in a long white beard on a throne,'" Dack recalled Gold telling her. "'It's that catch in your throat when you look out at the mountain—that's an experience of God.'" That fresh way of looking at the Divine helped Dack overcome what had felt like "uninspiring" experiences in synagogues. She began to forge a positive relationship with Judaism and with the "mysterious force" that she now believes fills the world. "For me, God is an energy force that pervades the entire universe within us, around us," said Dack. "There's a force of guidance. There is a pull toward goodness and toward sanctity when we tap in—and when we don't, we can fall. There's a sense of being held, supported, inspired, and guided."

In a concrete way, Dack's evolving beliefs led her to shift her basic attitudes, from an emphasis on accumulating material possessions to a focus on building a meaningful life. She found herself looking at the people around her differently, seeking out substance rather than style. And her parenting changed, as she strove to communicate her new values to her daughters. "I used to judge people in a shallow way, based on their appearance," Dack said. "I didn't want my children to discount extraordinary people because they didn't have the latest hairdo or they weren't driving a flashy car." She sought to live and to teach her family the importance of avoiding *lashon hara*, the idle gossip that can damage reputations and diminish the inherent dignity of others.

Yet, for a significant number of Jews, belief in God remains a question mark or a distant metaphor. Though Sandra Lash harbors religious doubts, she plays an active role

in her synagogue, serving on its spiritual life committee, helping to organize special events, and taking part in Torah study.
Indeed, she connects to Judaism through its sacred texts—
even if her interpretations sidestep traditional understandings.
"I enjoy reading the Torah and delving into it," Lash said. "It
represents early human wisdom and living by laws, as opposed
to the whim of the powerful." This moral framework echoes
the ideals she learned as a child in a secular Sephardic family.
"I grew up with all these values without the religion," said
Lash, noting that her moral code "didn't get tied to Judaism
until later, in adulthood." Today, Lash anchors her Jewish
practice in community building and ethics, keeping divinity
(and her doubts about it) in the background. "God is an idea I
can use as a metaphor," Lash said. "I think the idea of God
keeps us from being too narcissistic."

When the Torah seems likes a distant document from
times far different from our own, fictional re-creations of that
world sometimes have the power to make it live. Anita
Diamant's novel *The Red Tent* imagines the lives of some of the
Torah's female figures, such as Rachel and Leah, touched off a
series of dreams for Stephanie Ozer, a Northern California jazz
pianist. "All of a sudden, I was roaming the desert," said Ozer,
in the company of biblical characters with whom she had
never felt a kinship. "The feeling I got when I woke up was a
feeling of divinity in the women's cycles and intuition—a
microcosm of the Earth and the universe," Ozer said. "When
you're connecting your life to the Earth, moon, and stars, you
are naturally going from the micro to the macro" level.

Yet she continues to wrestle intellectually with a religious
tradition that was not part of her secular upbringing. Ozer has
moved to a spiritual posture of "believing nonbeliever." Along
with the imagery of *The Red Tent*, she has found a metaphor
for divinity in music. As early as age eight, while playing Bach,
she had the sense that the sounds she was making flowed from

something greater than her own talents. "I was a vessel for music that was coming from above," Ozer recalled. "When I'm truly open to that divine energy of music, that's what God is to me." A soulful performance, she believes, can transform, even heal, the listeners, and in its own way, contribute to *tikkun olam*.

But for other Jewish voyagers, God is alive and well in a number of guises. Seattle's Pinchas Zohav has transformed his notion of God from punitive to creative. Said Zohav, "I was able to move from God the parent judge to God the artistic creator," through conversations with other participants at Etz Chayyim, the Jewish retreat center, then in New York's Hudson Valley.

After exposure to an omnipotent God through his boyhood Talmud Torah, Zohav's vision of spirituality now assumes a significant amount of free will on the part of individuals. We create much of our own reality, he believes, by our decision to listen or to ignore the "still small voice" of God, which he compares to a radio broadcast channel. "Some of us learn to still the noise and apparent chaos of day-to-day living and to pay especial attention to Divine Radio," Zohav said. "I would assert that if we get quiet, take the time to tune in, that we will, at least in retrospect, enjoy lives full of opportunities for joy, love, and accomplishment."

Some seekers develop a definition of the Divine that is grounded in both Judaism and other spiritual traditions. As both a Jew and a Buddhist, Lou Weiss finds God in what he calls the Oneness of the universe. "There is a force in us and among us that is more than us, which is comforting," Weiss said. He suggests that his relationship with the Divine is not so much with a being, as perhaps a positive energy field. "Even in the way I put on my *kippah* or my *tallit*, it's not a deference," said Weiss. "It's more of an embrace."

Others argue that building a vital relationship with the Divine, however defined, requires coming to terms with one's relationships—and unresolved conflicts—with family members. Most people encounter their first authority figures, their first sources of a moral code, in their parents. And troubles in those primal relationships can presage problems with God, as well, suggests Rabbi Hava Pell. "People base their understanding of God on their first caregivers," Pell argued. "One of the things that needs to be deconstructed in order to have real intimacy with God is to tease [apart] what's the voice of Mom and Dad, and what's the voice of God."

Pell drew insight into the nature of God from her seminary studies of the ancient religions that surrounded Judaism at its inception. Unlike other Near Eastern creation myths, the God-human relationship in the Torah is "one of emotional intimacy, not a master-servant relationship," she found. "A covenant relationship, a *brit*, is a partnership agreement between unequal parties," Pell said. "As someone who didn't know what love or intimacy was, it showed me God created me in love and longing."

Over the years, Pell has moved far beyond the academic focus of her Reconstructionist training to a more intuitive sense of the Divine. "The kind of understanding that I have about God is very spiritual and very mystical," Pell said. "I know that I wanted to be as loving and open-hearted as I could be." Her move from congregational rabbi to bar and bat mitzvah coach has led her to probe the spiritual subtext of Jewish rituals as common as kindling the Shabbat candles on Friday evening. "We can all light Shabbat candles and all get something different out of it," said Pell. "To me, that's proof of God's perfection and infiniteness."

A loving, if sometimes reproachful, presence. A reminder to be humble. A creative source. A sense of awe on the mountaintops of life. The seekers in this book tell of wildly disparate experiences of God. Yet, for all their seeming variety, these accounts have a couple of things in common. Most describe a divinity far different than the biblical portrait of a sometimes vengeful personage who intervenes directly in human affairs. In that sense, they have developed a picture of God more in tune with modern adult lives than the one-dimensional authority figure that used to be the stock in trade of religious education. Second, and perhaps most important, the test of belief for many on these Jewish journeys lies in living differently than before they reclaimed religion. A renewed commitment to honesty. An effort to reflect as well as to work hard. An attempt to avoid the words that wound. A deeper attention to loved ones. These, for some on the Jewish road home, are among the fruits of faith.

16

A *Tallit* That Fits
Making a Jewish Life That Works

Out of a gritty political struggle in the late 1990s activist Margie Klein acquired a fresh perspective on Shabbat. Friends used to gather on Friday evenings at her group house near Yale University, to take stock of their drive for an affordable-housing ballot initiative. Klein pictured her Jewish forebears celebrating Shabbat in the desert. If they could find blessing amid privation and uncertainty about the future, couldn't she and her houseful of community activists? "Even when you're in difficult times, there is also an important practice of remembering what is good in ours lives," Klein said. "Even when we lose, the sunset is still beautiful; your cousin had a baby."

She devised a ritual to match the challenge. Just before the blessing over the wine, everyone around the table would share a redemptive moment or a highlight from the past week and pour a portion from their own cup into the communal *Kiddush* cup. "By the time it made its way around the circle, it was overflowing with blessings"—and wine, Klein said of the communal cup.

Like that brimming cup, spiritual journeys are metaphors. In real terms, they comprise a personal itinerary of places, people, books, and other sources of wisdom, with a lot of questions and perhaps a few answers along the way. In the ordinary lives of twenty-first century American Jews, such inner travels are rarely put into words. It often takes rituals—whether wholly traditional, invented, or a deft combination of old and new—to ground the journey.

A Shift in Rhythm

For many of the people profiled in this book, creating an island of spiritual focus through Shabbat observance is the heart of their Jewish practice. They highlight different aspects of the day—the renewal of putting work aside; the intensity of praying hard and long; the power of gathering with others for meals, services, and thoughtful conversation—but this weekly retreat from the routine remains a potent tool for their spiritual unfolding.

"For me, there's nothing as high and meaningful and exhilarating as leaving the week behind and getting ready to enter Shabbat," said psychologist-composer Norma Brooks, who looks forward to services at Temple Shalom in Chevy Chase, Maryland, and Shabbat dinner with close friends. She marks her entry into sacred time with the singing during the Friday evening Kabbalat Shabbat service of *"L'cha Dodi"* ("Come, My Friend"), a call to welcome the Sabbath bride envisioned by the Jewish mystics of medieval Safed in the land of Israel. "It's very moving, that place of welcoming the Sabbath bride," said Brooks, who recalls first hearing this song three decades ago at Beit Havurah, a Jewish communal house in Connecticut, where the imagery came to life for her. "It felt like people were really welcoming, letting the light in."

Richard Chused and his wife, Elizabeth, have made Shabbat the cornerstone of their Jewish observance. It's a time to enjoy friends and put work on hold, he says. "Observing Shabbat changes the rhythm of your life," said Chused. "By changing one day, you change the other six." In slowing down this way, he is countering the driven professional life of the nation's capital, where he makes his home. "Particularly in American culture, which is so driven by work and merchandising and television, to not do that stuff for one day is almost unpatriotic," Chused said.

Over the years, the Chuseds also began keeping kosher, in part, he says, to make it easier to invite observant friends from their Conservative synagogue to their home for meals. "We just fell into it by not eating pork and shellfish, and did a sort of kosher style, which means not mixing milk or meat," Chused said of their early attempts at *kashrut*. In time, he and his wife came to see the kosher laws as a statement of their values. "Being Jewish is not just a Shabbat thing," Chused said. "It's about integrating Judaism into your entire life. It's not just a one-day shot."

Since Judith Dack entered Judaism through the portal of the Jewish Renewal movement, she keeps the traditions that move her forward and leaves behind those that impede her journey. "I'm really great at editing out what's disempowering to me," Dack said. "I have my own translations." Yet this yoga teacher and Hebrew chant leader keeps the Sabbath as a core of her Jewish practice. "Shabbat is a retreat day," said Dack. "If everybody really took off the twenty-five hours to nurture their soul, what a world it would be!" From week to week, her approach ranges from a quasi-Orthodox *shomer Shabbos* (a strict observance of Sabbath restrictions) attitude to worldly activity, such as time with her daughter pursuing with what she calls "Shabbat consciousness." Said Dack, "I keep Shabbat, but without dogma." As a yoga teacher in the Jewish community, Dack strives to "help people find a doorway" and sees herself as an "alternative community builder" for disaffected Jews. She was once one of them.

Meanwhile, congregational leader turned spiritual director Rabbi Hava Pell helps individuals and groups find personal meaning in the rhythms of Jewish life. While guiding others, she has reached a new way of understanding the familiar rituals of Shabbat. "It's not the same candle blessing for me every week. It's not the same Shabbos," Pell said. "It's, what's God's intention for me this week?"

A Spiritual Reckoning

Sacred time follows seasonal as well as weekly rhythms across the Jewish calendar. In her professional life as a chiropractor, Margot Barnet is accustomed to tallying the vertebrae on a client's aching back, but come Passover she's counting the *omer* (literally, a measure of barley). This daily reckoning goes on for seven weeks until the Festival of Shavuot, accompanied by a special blessing on the eve of each of the forty-nine days, in what Barnet calls a "remarkably spiritual practice."

Why keep tabs, when a calendar could simply do it for us? Barnet subscribes to a mystical interpretation of the *omer* popular in Hasidic and Jewish Renewal circles. Each week, she reflects on a different *sefirah*, or divine emanation: *chesed* (kindness, mercy), *gevurah* (judgment, strength), *tiferet* (beauty), *netzach* (eternity, victory), *hod* (glory), *yesod* (foundation, ego), and *malchut* (kingdom), in that order. Contemplating each *sefirah* alone, then in tandem with each of the other six, she uses this practice as a tool for self-improvement.

By counting the *omer*, "I was really able to get somewhere with some of the qualities that are challenging for me," Barnet said. "There were times it gave me great insight." Her reflections over the past half dozen years have lent her a fresh understanding of *gevurah* in her life. "Rather than being a punitive discipline, it was an internal discipline that would protect me from destructive and self-destructive influences," Barnet realized.

For SaraHope Smith, reciting the daily blessings during this spring festival period puts her in touch with the urgent need for *tikkun olam*. "My whole being feels so in sync with the counting of the *omer*," Smith said. "If Passover is the New Year of redemption, there's so much healing this world has to do." A religious eclectic, she has gleaned insights into counting the *omer* from Hasidic Rabbi Efraim Yolles of Crown Heights in Brooklyn. "The journey from Passover to Shavuot is a journey of healing our souls—our individual souls, the souls of our people, and the little hidden bits of light in our world," Smith said.

For Philip Mandelkorn, who hews to both Judaism and the integral school of yoga, celebrating the Jewish festivals helps bring him closer to God. He points to mystical teachings that suggest the ineffable is more easily sensed at these points on the calendar. "If you want to add italics to your life, you can follow the Jewish sages and observe these holy times," said the Virginia financial advisor. "I find myself getting in touch with God's presence more fully and deeply [at festivals] than at other times."

Beyond the cycles of the Jewish seasons, Mandelkorn has pondered the deeper meanings of the Hebrew alphabet, using meditations on its letters as "pathways to more refined consciousness." At work on a book he calls the *Torah Gita*, a digest and commentary on the Five Books of Moses, he says he has lately surrounded himself with cutout forms of *yud, samekh,* and *feh*, the Hebrew letters that spell the name of the biblical Joseph. "Anything you focus your mind on for any length of time reveals its secrets," said Mandelkorn. "By using these Hebrew letters, I find doorways."

In the Jewish month of Elul, leading up to the High Holy Days, Rabbi Tsurah August often turns to a practice developed by Jewish mystic Nachman of Bratslav: breaking open the heart. The process, says August, is simple yet profound. She begins by going to a private place, in nature if possible, and tapping her heart while repeating, "I am breaking my heart open to you." Then she speaks freely, without any script or forethought, to see what may emerge. "Sometimes it's sadness, sometimes it's apathy, it could be joy, gratefulness," August said. "The heart really opens." As a hospice chaplain who must be there for others, this practice helps her do the same for herself. "It's very cleansing," August said. "It gives an opportunity to find what's hidden in the heart, but needs expression, needs light."

Many returning Jews flag Passover as the holiday that speaks most powerfully to them. "It's such a brilliantly constructed ritual," said August. "It includes all the senses, and everyone can be involved." In recent years, her seder has included contributions by her six-year-old grandson, Harry, who wrote and illustrated his own Haggadah, based largely on the ten plagues. This child-centered text has offered a "wonderful opportunity," says his rabbinic grandmother, to wrestle as a family with such existential problems as the nature of good, evil, and God. "These are the eternal questions, and each year, we're in a different place in our lives, grappling with these questions," August said.

Sandra Lash reclaims her Sephardic heritage at the Passover seder as she recreates heirloom dishes of Turkish Jewry, such as matzah spinach feta pie, eggplant pie, fried *binuelos* (fried matzah dumplings served with honey), and the traditional date *charoset*. Beyond the cultural wealth of family recipes, this mental health clinic director finds nuggets of psychological meaning in the Haggadah's tale of Hebrew exodus from Egyptian bondage. For Lash, the holiday is about "making choices—to leave or not to leave, to cross the sea or not to cross the sea," she said. "It challenges us on a contemporary level [about] what we would be willing to take risks for."

For his part, dancer Steve Weintraub has made a point to add his personal choreography to Jewish festivals, what he calls "the pageant of the year." When the September 11 terrorist attacks occurred, he was living with his partner in an artists' loft complex in Atlanta. As a personal response to the tragedy, Weintraub erected a large *sukkah* (a shelter used for the holiday of Sukkot) in the common area, which soon collected contributions of art from neighbors, Jewish and non-Jewish: blown glass, bits of sculpture, and more. "Everybody got into making this little shrine to the fragility of peace," Weintraub said.

As he finds creative ways to mark the holidays, he is actually acting in accordance with a time-honored Jewish value, *hiddur mitzvah*, the Jewish imperative to lend beauty to religious practice. His goal, said Weintraub, is "to beautify the holidays in my own way and make them personally meaningful and meaningful to the people who come."

Like Weintraub, many returning Jews feel a need to put religious customs into new context. In this way, some Jewish women are re-creating the institution of the *mikvah*. Ann Kline uses it to mark passages in her life. "I love going to the *mikvah*," said Kline, although she does not follow the traditional family purity laws. "I go at least twice a year, once before the High Holy Days and once at my birthday." Connie Songer, the woman who discovered her Jewish heritage in her thirties, went to the *mikvah* with her daughters to mark their entry into Jewish life.

For their part, many men in liberal corners of the Jewish world are reclaiming the practice of donning *tefillin*. Lloyd Wolf's path led this secular-bred, worldly artist to don these visual symbols of Jewish commitment. "I'm not as regular with *tefillin*, but I travel with them," says Wolf, whose photography work has taken him around the world. These emblems of prayer represent for him the continual opportunity for a connection with the Divine. "The core of Judaism is the direct relationship with God," says Wolf. "There's no intermediary. It's up to you and God."

Ann Kline uses storytelling as a practice that can shine a light on Jewish values for both teller and listeners. "You tell a story to teach yourself," said Kline. Her favorite, from David Lieb, involves a student of the Ba'al Shem Tov who traveled to study with the great Hasidic master. Villagers along the way stop him, begging him to be the tenth person in their minyan. He declines, intent on joining his teacher. Yet, when the student approaches the Ba'al Shem Tov after services, the teacher does not shake his hand and reproaches him for not joining the minyan en route.

For Kline, the lesson of this tale lies in how the student, obsessed with his destination, fails to seize opportunity when it hovers in his face. It's about "how we miss the richness of our life because we're always looking somewhere else, that every moment provides us with the opportunity, the invitation to be fully ourselves," Kline said.

As she weaves together a life as rabbi, professor, and spiritual director, Rabbi Leila Gal Berner has adopted a practice—often unseen by anyone else—that helps her place her varied roles on a larger loom. "Whenever I study, teach, or am doing anything I consider of a sacred nature—if I'm writing a *d'var Torah* or doing an audio teleconference teaching by phone in my pajamas to students around the world—I wear my *kippah*," said Berner. "It's a way for me to remind myself that I'm doing *avodat kodesh*, sacred work."

Before she delves into Jewish texts or interprets them to audiences near or far, she also turns to the traditional *Birkat Limud Torah* (Blessing for Torah Study) to recall the greater purpose underlying the task at hand. Indeed, she says, the last three words of the blessing, *"la'asok b'divrei Torah,"* can translate as "to be engaged with words of Torah." What that really means, from where Berner sits, is "take them in organically, so you live them, so the words of Torah become tools for living rather than just for thinking."

Every religion develops its own set of tools in order to cultivate and nurture spiritual experiences. Christians renew their faith through the act of Communion, the taking of wafer and wine. Muslims surrender to God as they pray five times daily. Jews can draw on their own rich store of practices designed to bring holiness into daily life, ranging from Shabbat and its blessings, to *tefillin* and *mikvah*, to the year's round of festivals, from the introspective High Holy Days to the liberation story of the Passover seder.

Yet, as they reclaim these traditions, many seekers find they must reframe them, in order to strengthen their original purpose. What is customary can become stale, and repetition without *kavanah* (intention) can rob ceremony of its soul. Sometimes, as with Margie Klein's *Kiddush* variation and other examples in this chapter, the re-creation of ritual keeps its spirit alive and helps Judaism speak to new generations.

17 Circle at Sinai
Community Questions

Talk to more than five dozen American Jews in search of a workable spirituality—women and men, coast to coast, outside the liberal denominations and sometimes inside of them—and some patterns begin to emerge. The people profiled in the preceding chapters each tell a story singular in its details, but bearing common landmarks, pathways, walls, and entrances, as well as moments of exultation and despair. One person's disenchantment with Jewish life may stem from individual spiritual longings and frustrations, colored by family background, access to vibrant education, and opportunities for engagement with a Jewish community. Yet, when scores of Jews come close to losing their religious heritage along the way, as is true of many I interviewed, their experiences hint at an unknowable number of others who remain outside the pale.

An avalanche of attrition silently peels estimated thousands away from the Jewish community year after year. The stories of the returnees, and in some cases, their lingering ambivalence, may suggest larger problems worth attention and solutions. Take one marker of religious vitality or stagnation: Passover.

Studies suggest that many Jews at the margins observe this holiday even if they do little else that is tangibly Jewish. Yet, in the two decades since I fell in love with Pesach, I have sat at too many seders where few people knew the songs of the Haggadah, one of the most profound pieces of sacred musical theater ever written. Even fewer seemed to draw personal meaning from this great tale of liberation, which celebrates the struggle against oppression and teaches compassion for our adversaries. These disconnects do not reflect on those with whom I've broken matzah, whose company I treasured. The silences at the seder table speak, instead, to the yawning gap between practice and relevance that rives our community today.

With the voices of more than sixty Jewish seekers still ringing in my ears, let me sketch some themes of their stories that may interest Jewish communal leaders, educators, and others concerned with the well-being of the Jewish community. They jibe with my own experiences and those of others I have met during a decade in Jewish journalism.

Tradition Intrigues, but Meaning Matters More

In the classic musical *Fiddler on the Roof*, a chorus of townspeople from the shtetl of Anatevka describe their community in the musical number "Tradition." The song's lyrics offer no larger reason for the town's folkways than the sheer weight of religious and cultural habit. For some American Jews, similar appeals to heritage tug at their hearts and inspire loyalty. For others, custom for custom's sake does not suffice. The people profiled here value Jewish traditions. But, in varying degrees, they spent years viewing them as irrelevant and hollow, or as remote from twenty-first-century lives as Tevye the milkman's horse-drawn cart. Frequently, rote formulations of Jewish beliefs, rituals, and *mitzvot* fail to feed their souls. Yet they are hungry for a larger context of meaning—practical, mystical, social, personal, or all of the above. What does Judaism ask of us in the workplace? In our families, especially as we care for our children and elders? What do our beliefs mean for the causes we espouse? For the sense of greater purpose in which we seek to enfold our own lives? Jewish institutions that address these question will become more relevant to more American Jews.

Israel Can Inspire People, but They Still Need Spiritual Community at Home

Travels to the Jewish state offer participants, especially young people, a sense of Jewish peoplehood and history. Some have told me of early experiments in religious observance that flowed out of their tours or studies in Israel. Yet for many of those interviewed, visiting Israel did not address their spiritual quandaries. That required finding the right mentors, teachers, and spiritual communities to nurture a Jewish identity on their home turf. Both Pinchas Zohav and Rabbi Leila Gal Berner, to cite two examples, lived for years in Israel, but they had to discover welcoming congregations and spirited services back in the United States before they could enjoy the religious side of their Jewish identities.

Trips to Israel may bond Jews to their heritage, but they still have to find how it fits into their lives afterward. As we saw in earlier chapters, the dancer has to dance, the activist to organize, the parent to guide and love, the ill person to heal; for all the challenges of every phase of life and field of work, discovering a spiritual dimension can enlarge horizons. This is, ultimately, an inside job. Visiting the Jewish homeland can help, but the work of creating a Jewish home and community remains.

Education Must Link Jewish Teachings and Lived Experience

I have reported on and benefited from inspired Jewish teachers, and hold them in high esteem. Yet, if there was a near-universal thread to my conversations with Jewish seekers across the generations, it was a loathing of Hebrew school and other religious education for young people. Adult education, on the other hand, tended to get high marks. Inspiration and personal connection seem to be missing in the way our children are learning about Judaism. New pedagogies that stress the experiential and that appeal to different learning styles have the potential to help. The education that lasts, I believe, will forge connections between real life and Jewish ideals. It will address, in age-appropriate ways, the thirst for meaning expressed by so many adults as they look back on what often feels like the spiritual wastelands of their early years.

Ann Kline could have been describing Jewish education when she cited an approach she has found useful in helping others examine their spiritual path. They need help "reframing stories and rituals in ways that are less rote," Kline said. "You can break open the ritual to find your place in it—not to reject the community story, but to make it your own." To listen to Kline and others like her, American Jews need more encouragement from teachers not simply to master Hebrew or Jewish history, but to draw their own lessons on the journey of learning.

Spirituality Crosses Jewish Denominational Lines

Eighteen of the sixty-two people profiled in this book called themselves "post-denominational" Jews, belonged to two different kinds of Jewish congregations, or were clearly influenced by more than one part of the Jewish religious spectrum. They are crafting a Jewish identity that's bigger than any synagogue or denominational movement can hold. They seem more passionate about a meaningful Jewish life than about sectarian differences.

Younger adults voice the loudest disenchantment with religious divisions. Environmental activist Jeremy Manela surveys his peers in their twenties and sees most of them leaping denominational fences. "In my generation, certainly, I've met a few people who are into their [movement's] youth group, but the majority are interested in finding their own way through Jewish tradition, not one school of thought," he said. The young adults he knows trust their guts—and each other—more than the dictates and customs of organized Jewry. "We don't look to established institutions or authorities to tell us how to live spiritually," Manela said. "It's choose your own adventure—with friends, collectively, communally."

Like a number of those profiled in this book, biochemist turned novelist Maggie Anton has found more than one home for her Jewish soul. She and her husband joined both a Conservative and a Reform synagogue. Anton says she feels more in tune with the ritual "practice" in a Conservative context, but closer to Reform "ideology." In a similar vein, Ukrainian-born Natasha Hirschhorn attended a nondenominational cantorial school. "I felt sad limiting myself to one form of Judaism," Hirschhorn said. "I felt as if I would be locking myself in." Late-blooming Jews, it seems, identify more with the whole community than with its divisions.

Geography Shapes Jewish Needs

The Jewish establishment focuses on the largest U.S. urban centers, while it sometimes forgets about how Jews outside those areas really live. Now living outside Syracuse, New York, Ruth Kurlandsky long made her home in Grand Rapids, Michigan, where Jews are a tiny minority. She recalls representatives from the Conservative movement who would tout The Jewish Theological Seminary, but who "never mentioned Camp Ramah," not realizing that for Jews in the hinterlands, the nearest Jewish summer camp played a much greater role than the seminary in transmitting values from generation to generation. In low-density Jewish areas, from the Midwest to the Southwest and Southeast, finding or building vibrant

Jewish communities for young and old is a prerequisite for Jewish survival. Comments from other Jews in North Carolina and New Mexico bolstered Kurlandsky's observations.

Jewish Practice Must Offer Joy, Meaning, and Community—Perfection Is Not Required

As they gain some measure of peace with their own wounds and struggles, Jewish seekers tend to take a more generous view of Jewish life, in all its contradictions. "People who have been paralyzed or tortured or fearful toward Judaism find a piece, a spark, or something joyful or complete—even in the brokenness of how they were taught or raised," observed filmmaker Erik Greenberg Anjou. Anjou sees the complexities of spiritual life mirrored in the imagery of darkness and light— "an instrumental part of Jewish liturgy." These visual metaphors reflect what he sees as the essential loneliness of each person's religious journey, apart from communal gatherings. "The way Jews have created a structure through prayer, through ritual, is a brilliant system that allows for expressing grief, wrenching pain, wrestling with God, and incredible moments of celebration and ecstasy," Anjou said, "but where Judaism can't always succeed—there's a giant gap between the communal and systemic, and the personal." Even with group support, individuals have to find their own spiritual path. "There's a place you can go for minyan and get a hug, but at the end of the day, you're alone and you have to deal with it," Anjou said.

Spiritual Polygamy Lives

For many wandering Jews, reclaiming their religious heritage is not an all-or-nothing proposition. They have a foot in the Jewish world and another in what they see as a complementary spiritual discipline, such as yoga, tai chi, or meditation. Clearly some traditions, such as Christianity, Hinduism, and

Islam, entail beliefs and practices at odds with Judaism. Jewish integrity does not permit a religious fusion with these faiths. Groups that purport to espouse both Jewish trappings and the divinity of Jesus, for example, have some explaining to do. Yet some forms of spiritual polygamy are here to stay, and like it or not, Jewish leaders may have better odds of reaching those at the margins by recognizing their other spiritual interests, rather than pretending they don't exist.

Raised a Conservative Jew in rural Ohio, Lou Weiss walked back into Jewish life through the door of Reconstructionism, initially impelled by a daughter's religious curiosity. Yet, in recent years, Weiss has grafted another spiritual tradition onto his roots: Buddhism. In particular, he has followed his second wife into a *sangha*, or community, based on the teachings of Vietnamese-French monk Thich Nhat Hanh, who strikes this psychologist as a "Reconstructionist Buddhist."

His espousal of the wisdom of Hanh, who stresses worldly activism for justice as well as mindful living, has not made Weiss reject Judaism. "Everything we read we take back to our native language," Weiss said. "I realized that the more I became immersed in the Buddhism, the stronger I felt toward my Judaism." In recent years, that means you can find him at the Torah study and Reconstructionist minyan on Saturday morning—during a Shabbat he cleared of client appointments years ago—and at the *sangha* on Sunday evening. In this dual spiritual life, he is hardly alone among American Jews.

Green Values Draw Jews

The environmental side of Judaism holds special appeal for some baby boomers and many younger Jews. The spiritual leader of a Maryland synagogue built upon green principles, Rabbi Fred Scherlinder Dobb, has heard congregants tell him that they would only join a congregation that cares about its ecological footprint. "Many Jews need alignment between their beautiful faith and spiritual community, on the one hand, and their deeply held commitments in the public sphere, on the other other," Dobb said.

In this light, Jewish institutions have much to gain when they are crafting policies and programs, by drawing on such values inherent in Judaism as kindness to living things. Doing the right thing, environmentally speaking, is likely to draw people for whom these issues deeply matter.

Jewish Arts Create Pathways for Spiritual Growth

The worlds of music, storytelling, calligraphy, and more have offered routes into a richer Jewish life for many people. As wise teachers know, not everyone learns best through text-based, cerebral methods. For those with a bent for visual art, for example, the challenge of making art based on Hebrew letters can send them on a journey of exploration into the meaning of these symbols. The impact of such experiences does not stop with artists but ripples out to their audiences, particularly in the performing arts. This can be seen at any high-energy klezmer concert or challenging Jewish play.

Creative Margins Feed the Mainstream

Jews in the religious establishment draw sustenance from such centers of spiritual ferment as Elat Chayyim Center for Jewish Spirituality and the Chavurah Institute. A striking number of dues-paying synagogue members also take part in institutions like these. There really is no *mechitza*, no firm dividing line between these two worlds, which serve different needs, at different stages of a spiritual journey. What some institutions and communal leaders may see as marginal Jewish activity—such as a nondenominational retreat on Hebrew chanting or Judaic storytelling—is actually what makes it possible for a significant number of people to remain a part of the Jewish community. For that reason, these creative margins deserve communal support.

Judaism Is Poised to Make a Larger Impact on the National Debate about Values

Simon Greer, of the Jewish Funds for Justice, sees a vestige of European ghettos—whose forbidding walls may have encouraged an insular outlook—in the defensive posture of some Jewish groups now. Argued Greer, "It's ironic that our leadership would sometimes return us to cul-de-sac Judaism, when our victories and successes have won us the right to the town square."

From another berth in the Jewish world, spiritual director Ann Kline laments what she sees as the Jewish absence in general audience spiritual books and in the public dialogue on spirituality. "The kind of protective mechanisms that helped us when we were children aren't necessarily the best strategies for us as adults," Kline said. "By extension, that's true for a culture." It's time, she believes, for Judaism to show a more public and expansive face, to address new questions: "How do we live our Jewish values in the wider world, and how do we share those values?"

For his part, Greer predicts serving local communities will become a rite of passage for young American Jews over the next decade. "If service is an expression of Judaism that does good in the world, that creates meaningful reflection on Jewish values and is a pathway into the town square—if that's what Judaism brings into their lives, then of course they'd want a Jewish identity," Greer said.

Their observations point to the need for institutional change on two levels. First, the Jewish world needs to blaze pathways for community service grounded in Jewish values available to teens and young adults across the country. The American Jewish World Service; PANIM: The Institute for

Jewish Leadership and Values; and Hazon have developed templates for these kinds of programs. And second, Jewish communal leaders have an obligation to join the national conversation on spirituality at conferences in and out of the Jewish world, in publications, and in the blogosphere. There are people out there waiting to hear authentic Jewish voices that address the widespread hunger for spiritual meaning. Their words could touch lives.

18

Kissing the
Mezuzah
Lessons of the Journey

Moses, the Torah relates, strode up a mountaintop to receive the Jewish laws from God. Early on, he harbored doubts about his fitness as a leader, but he raised no major questions about the moral code he bore downslope on clay tablets.

Today, most of us are less decisive and far less confident in our pursuit of spiritual wisdom. The landscape of our journeys resembles less a rocky peak we can climb than an earthen path that meanders like an old streambed, with loops that double back to nearly touch each other. We gain insight only to lose it around the next bend. We learn a vital lesson and then grow distracted before translating idea into action. Our interests shift. We crash from hope to despair, and slowly rise again in a tide of unexpected joy. Sometimes, such upheavals as a new romance, the birth of a child, the death of a loved one, or a shift in careers power our spiritual growth. Yet we can also feel an inner transformation touched off by nothing more than a moment of wonder, when we find unexpected blessing in a friendly word, a soaring bird, a sky full of stars, or a common cause.

Others have walked this winding road. In your own Jewish explorations, you may find value in trying one or two of the routes that have moved them forward. The following are some spiritual compass points suggested by the experiences of the people in this book.

Spiritual Journey Checklist

1. **Keep a journal.** Record your inner life to better see its patterns and the potential for further spiritual growth. Note the character traits you wish to strengthen, build, or alter.

2. **Meditate.** For twenty minutes a day or whatever time you can manage, focus on your breath. Give the process a Jewish spin by inwardly repeating with each inhalation or exhalation a Hebrew letter, word, or phrase, such as *shalom* (peace), that you find meaningful.

3. **Read.** Design a Jewish reading list to pursue alone or, even better, with a study partner. Explore Torah, Jewish history, Yiddish fiction, or modern Israeli poetry.

4. **Share Shabbat.** Light candles and recite the blessings over wine and challah with family and friends. Make a special meal. Sing. Put the workweek behind you and enjoy conversation about things that matter.

5. **Say a *b'racha* (blessing).** Use Hebrew, English, or any combination of languages that engage you. Voice gratitude for life's moments of wonder, whether it's meeting an old friend, glimpsing a gorgeous sunset, or winning a small victory in the struggle for *tikkun olam* (repairing the world).

6. **Do a *mitzvah* for someone else.** Offer an elderly person a ride to shul or shopping. Visit a sick friend or family member. Take care of a child who's not your own.

7. **Adopt a tradition.** Learn a prayer, such as the morning *Modeh/Modah Ani* or the Friday evening *Kiddush*. Give it your own interpretation. What does the restoration of your soul or liberation from slavery mean to you on your journey? Add your personal touch to the lighting of Shabbat candles or the Passover seder, whether it's a poem, a song, or a blessing you wrote for your children or your beloved.

8. **Parent with *ruach* (spirit).** Devise your own ways to teach your child Jewish values. For ideas, read Wendy Mogel's *The Blessing of a Skinned Knee*, or *Parenting as a Spiritual Journey: Deepening Ordinary and Extraordinary Events into Sacred Occasions* by Rabbi Nancy Fuchs-Kreimer (Jewish Lights). For more resources see p. 182.

9. **Find nurture in nature.** Focus on the beauty of creation. Or try Nachman of Breslov's "breaking open the heart" exercise (see chapter 16 for details).

10. **Take it to work.** Apply Jewish ethics to your job or business. Make one decision with that in mind—with a healthy respect for the ethical beliefs of your co-workers! Browse Wayne Dosick's *The Business Bible: 10 New Commandments for Bringing Spirituality & Ethical Values into the Workplace* (Jewish Lights); Nathan Laufer's *The Genesis of Leadership: What the Bible Teaches Us about Vision, Values and Leading Change* (Jewish Lights); Norman Cohen's *Moses and the Journey to Leadership: Timeless Lessons of Effective Management from the Bible and Today's Leaders* (Jewish Lights); *A Jewish Perspective* by Moses L. Pava; or *Values, Prosperity, and the Talmud* by Larry Kahaner.

11. **Explore the Jewish arts.** Learn klezmer or Sephardic music. Try your hand at Hebrew calligraphy. Or adapt one of your existing skills—from sewing to carving to writing—to Jewish themes.

12. **Find a teacher.** Locate someone in your community who can guide your studies of Hebrew, Jewish history, Torah, or other interests.

13. **Put your money where your values are.** If you're not already in the habit of giving *tzedakah* to worthy causes, make it part of your monthly check-writing routine. Jewish tradition suggests that we give at least ten percent of our income to help others.

14. **Rediscover Jewish flavors.** Try your hand at a family or cookbook recipe such as matzah ball soup, honey cake, Persian *fesenjan* (fowl with walnut-pomegranate sauce), or Italian *melanzane con melone* (fried eggplant with cantaloupe chunks).

15. **Cull the *parshah*.** Make time to read the weekly Torah portion. Identify one verse, narrative, or character that relates to your spiritual journey.

16. **Sift a story.** Read or recite a Jewish story from the folk or Hasidic tradition. How does it relate to the choices with which you are grappling on your own journey? Good sources for stories include *The Classic Tales* by Ellen Frankel and books by Howard Schwartz, such as *Tree of Souls* and *Gabriel's Palace*.

17. **Connect with a congregation.** *Daven* or study with others. Find at least one way to give back to the community.

18. **Form a discussion group.** Find others who are interested in sharing experiences from their spiritual journeys.

This chapter began with a disclaimer. In our spiritual quests, most of us act less like Moses and more like a hiker unsure of the trail ahead. Yet all of us also carry in our spiritual backpacks the potential for deep wisdom and for metamorphosis as radical as a larva turning into a butterfly. We have seen in the preceding stories how people can powerfully transform their lives: a skeptical scientist turns witness to the Divine, a Communist stalwart evolves into a Jewish storyteller, a high-tech executive becomes a rabbi. Some, perhaps most, spiritual journeys involve changes in miniature—a kinder atmosphere at home, a more contemplative work commute or lunch break, a new volunteer commitment, or a financial contribution to a community cause. Such small steps forward may be hard to perceive. Indeed, they may remain undetectable to anyone but the travelers themselves. Yet they can bring a measure of peace, an ounce of celebration to life's triumphs and challenges. And they can infuse our days with meaning.

"If you create a narrative for your life of an epic spiritual journey, you can wind up living one," said social justice activist Margie Klein, who, in her late twenties, has already traveled far. For some of us, borrowing that sense of grandeur can lift the spirits. It may help us draw a wider horizon on what may feel like the cramped picture of our daily existence. For others of us, it may make more sense to zoom in on the details of our lives, to better see where a renewed spirituality can touch our bonds with others, or help us better our communities, and ultimately, life on Earth.

Some can envision their journey as an epic soul trek. Others picture it as a series of small incremental steps toward living closer to God and our highest values. Whatever the scope of your own wanderings, know that you do not travel alone. Your companions are legion—in the next town and across a continent, alive today or nestled in Jewish history—even if you may not always know their names. Perhaps you have found a kindred *neshama* or two in the pages of this book. Jewish tradition teaches that the choices we make can create ripples far beyond our lives. We seek holiness, not only for its own sake, but for the sake of repairing the world. History—from antiquity through the Holocaust to last week's news report—and contemporary lives offer ample evidence of the power of people, alone and together, to heal or harm those around them. A host of passages from the Torah and the Talmud undergird this teaching. My personal favorite, which hangs framed in the foyer of my home, is this saying by the first-century Jewish Sage, Hillel: "If I am not for myself, who is for me? And if I am only for myself, what am I? And if not now, when?"

Wherever the road takes you, may you go from strength to strength.

Glossary

aliyah: Literally, "ascent"; refers to the blessing before the Torah reading at a Jewish service; also used to mean a move to the State of Israel.

Ashkenazic: Referring to Central and Eastern European Jewry.

ba'al teshuvah: Literally, "master of the return," alluding to liberal or secular Jews who reclaim a traditional or Orthodox Judaism.

bashert: Destiny or fate.

bimah: The altar of a synagogue sanctuary.

b'rit milah: The rite of circumcision.

b'racha: A blessing.

challah cover: A decorative cloth used to cover the traditional braided loaf before it is removed for the blessing over bread recited on Shabbat Eve.

chavurah: A Jewish worship group led by participants.

chevra: Jewish social circle or friendship group.

chevruta: Study partner.

Chumash: A volume containing the first five books of the Bible, plus excerpts from the Prophets; used in Saturday- morning services.

daven: To fervently pray.

d'var Torah: Literally, "a word of Torah"; a sermon or oral commentary on the Hebrew Bible.

Eyn Sof: A Kabbalist concept of God as infinite (literally, "without end").

Haggadah: A traditional or modern "script" of prayers and readings for the Passover seder.

Halacha: Body of Jewish law that forms the legal part of the Talmud.

Halachic: Referring to Halacha, or Jewish law.

hamantaschen: Literally, "Haman's hat"; a triangle-shaped pastry, associated with the Purim holiday, which is traditionally filled with poppy seeds, prunes, or apricots.

Hasidism, Hasidic: Referring to a Jewish movement that dates to the eighteenth century and stresses an ecstatic style of worship.

Havdalah: The bittersweet ceremony that closes the Shabbat, which includes the smelling of spices and the dousing of a braided candle in a cup of wine.

hazzanut, hazzanes (plural): Traditional cantorial styling.

heymish: Cozy, intimate.

Kaddish: A prayer said by mourners that praises God and speaks of peace, but does not mention death; it is traditionally recited in a minyan of ten adult Jews or more.

kashrut: Jewish kosher or dietary laws.

kavanah: Intention; focus with regard to prayer or ritual.

ketubah, ketubot (plural): Marriage contract.

kippah, kippot (plural): Skullcap worn by men and some women in Jewish settings; also known as a *yarmulke*.

maggid: Storyteller, especially in the Hasidic and Jewish Renewal movements.

mechitza: Partition that separates men and women in some synagogues.

mezuzah, mezuzot (plural): A small, rectangular box, often decorative, which contains a scroll with verses from the *Shema* prayer and is placed on the doorpost of a house and many of its rooms.

mikvah: A ritual bath or pool, used by women for purification ceremonies and by people of both genders to mark their conversion to Judaism.

minhag: Custom.

minyan: A Jewish quorum of ten needed to say certain prayers, such as the mourner's *Kaddish*.

Mi Shebeirach: Literally, "the One who blessed"; a prayer beginning with those words used in congregations for occasions of gratitude, celebration, and healing, including being called to the Torah and marking a wedding or anniversary; sometimes refers to the prayer of healing for the sick.

mitzvah, mitzvot (plural): Holy deeds or obligations, such as visiting the sick, comforting the bereaved, and assisting the needy, as well as ritual practices, such as observing Shabbat and the Jewish holidays.

ner tamid: Eternal light, referring to a light kept burning continuously above the ark in a synagogue sanctuary as a symbol of the ancient Temple's ever-burning seven-branched menorah and God's presence.

neshama: One of several Hebrew words for soul.

nusach: Cantorial styles developed for particular Jewish holidays, notably Rosh Hashanah and Yom Kippur.

Pidyon HaBen: Literally, "redemption of the firstborn son"; a ritual that redeems a firstborn son from dedication to God; celebrated thirty days after the baby's birth, it involves payment of five shekels (commonly five dollars in change) by the father to a member of the Jewish priestly class.

pushke: Container designated for collecting money for philanthropies; also known as a *tzedakah* box.

ruach: Spirit.

sefer: Book.

Sephardic: Related to Jews whose family origins are traceable to medieval Spain.

shalom bayit: Literally, "peace in the home"; the Jewish value of domestic harmony.

shivah: Traditional seven-day mourning period observed in Jewish homes.

shivah minyan: Gathering, often including a special religious service, in the home of a deceased person or mourner, held in the week after a death.

shofar: Ram's horn blown during High Holy Day services.

shomer Shabbat, shomer Shabbos: Literally, "guardian of the Sabbath"; a person who follows Sabbath restrictions on work and travel.

shul: Synagogue.

shule: School.

siddur, siddurim (plural): Prayer book.

simcha: A happy occasion; usually denotes a joyous life-cycle event, such as a wedding or a bar/bat mitzvah.

s'micha: Rabbinic ordination.

sukkah: A shelter or hut, usually set up outdoors for the harvest festival of Sukkot.

tallit or *tallis, tallitot* or *tallesim* (plural): Prayer shawl worn traditionally by men, and increasingly, by women in the liberal streams of Judaism.

tefillin or phylacteries: Small leather boxes, enclosing Hebrew scrolls and attached to leather straps, worn over the brow and forearm as a symbol of commitment by observant Jewish men and some women for weekday morning prayers.

tikkun olam: Repairing the world; an idea rooted in the Jewish mystical idea of vessels of light shattered at creation that require repair through the performance of *mitzvot*, often interpreted as acts of social justice.

tish: Table.

tzedakah: Justice or philanthropy.

tzedakah box: Container designated for collecting money for philanthropies; also known as a *pushke*.

tzitzit: Knotted fringe of the *tallit,* symbolizing the 613 *mitzvot* set forth in the Torah.

yahrzeit: The anniversary of a death, especially of a loved one.

yarmulke: Skullcap used by men and some women in Jewish settings; also known as a *kippah*.

yasher koach: Literally, "may you be strengthened," or more loosely, more power to you; blessing or congratulatory phrase said to someone who has just played a ritual, ceremonial, or educational role in the Jewish community.

Yiddishkeit: Jewish culture from the Eastern European tradition.

Yizkor: Literally, "remember"; memorial service used to recall deceased loved ones, held during four major holidays: Yom Kippur, the eighth day of Sukkot (Shemini Atzeret), Passover, and the second day of Shavuot.

Suggestions for Further Reading

Here is a small sample from the wealth of Jewish resources available in bookstores and online. Some of these titles have fueled my own spiritual journey. Every reader is different. Find the books that translate the wisdom of Judaism into a language that speaks to you. Explore and enjoy!

Family Life

Abramowitz, Yosef I. and Rabbi Susan Silverman. *Jewish Family & Life: Traditions, Holidays, and Values for Today's Parents and Children*. New York: Golden Books, 1997.

Adelman, Penina, Ali Feldman and Shulamit Reinharz. *The JGirl's Guide: The Young Jewish Woman's Handbook for Coming of Age*. Woodstock, VT: Jewish Lights, 2005.

Doades, Joanne. *Parenting Jewish Teens: A Guide for the Perplexed*. Woodstock, VT: Jewish Lights, 2006.

Feinstein, Edward. *Tough Questions Jews Ask: A Young Adult's Guide to Building a Jewish Life*. Woodstock, VT: Jewish Lights, 2003.

Mogel, Wendy. *The Blessing of a Skinned Knee: Using Jewish Teachings to Raise Self-Reliant Children*. Middlesex, UK: Penguin Books, 2001.

Olitzky, Kerry M., and Daniel Judson, eds. *The Rituals & Practices of a Jewish Life: A Handbook for Personal Spiritual Renewal*. Woodstock, VT: Jewish Lights, 2002.

Hebrew and Torah

Falk, Marcia. *The Book of Blessings*. New York: HarperCollins, 1996.

Samuel, Edith. *Your Jewish Lexicon: Some Words and Phrases in Jewish Life and Thought in Hebrew and English*. New York: Urj Press, 1982.

Telushkin, Joseph. *Biblical Literacy: The Most Important People, Events, and Ideas of the Hebrew Bible*. New York: William Morrow, 1997.

Jewish Practice

Diamant, Anita and Howard Cooper. *Living a Jewish Life: Jewish Traditions, Customs and Values for Today's Families*. New York: HarperCollins, 1991.

Cohen, Norman J. *Moses and the Journey to Leadership: Timeless Lessons of Effective Management from the Bible and Today's Leaders.* Woodstock, VT: Jewish Lights, 2006.

Dosick, Wayne. *The Business Bible: 10 New Commandments for Bringing Spirituality & Ethical Values into the Workplace.* Woodstock, VT: Jewish Lights, 2000.

Heschel, Abraham J. *The Sabbath.* New York: Farrar, Straus and Giroux, 1951.

Kahaner, Larry. *Values, Prosperity, and the Talmud: Business Lessons from the Ancient Rabbis.* Hoboken, NJ: John Wiley & Sons, 2003.

Laufer, Nathan. *The Genesis of Leadership: What the Bible Teaches Us about Vision, Values and Leading Change.* Woodstock, VT: Jewish Lights, 2006.

Pava, Moses L. *Business Ethics: A Jewish Perspective.* Jersey City, NJ: KTAV, 1997.

Schachter-Shalomi, Zalman and Joel Segel. *Jewish With Feeling: A Guide to Meaningful Jewish Practice.* New York: Riverhead Books, 2005.

Shapiro, Rami. *Minyan: Ten Principles for Living a Life of Integrity.* New York: Bell Tower, 1997.

Telushkin, Joseph. *The Book of Jewish Values: A Day-by-Day Guide to Ethical Living.* New York: Bell Tower, 2000.

Waskow, Arthur. *Seasons of Our Joy: A Modern Guide to the Jewish Holidays.* Boston: Beacon Press, 1991.

Jewish Stories
Murphy, Claire Rodolf, Meghan Nuttall Sayres, Mary Cronk Farrell, Sarah Conover, and Betsy Wharton. *Daughters of the Desert: Stories of Remarkable Women from Christian, Jewish and Muslim Traditions.* Woodstock, VT: SkyLight Paths, 2005.

Nachman of Breslov. Trans. by Aryeh Kaplan. *The Lost Princess & Other Kabbalistic Tales of Rebbe Nachman of Breslov.* Woodstock, VT: Jewish Lights, 2007.

———. *The Seven Beggars & Other Kabbalistic Tales of Rebbe Nachman of Breslov.* Woodstock, VT: Jewish Lights, 2005.

Frankel, Ellen. *The Classic Tales: 4,000 Years of Jewish Lore.* Lanham, MD: Jason Aronson, 1989.

Schwarz, Howard. *Gabriel's Palace: Jewish Mystical Tales.* London: Oxford University Press, 1993.

———. *Tree of Souls: The Mythology of Judaism.* London: Oxford University Press, 2005.

Judaism and the Environment

Benstein, Jeremy. *The Way Into Judaism and the Environment.* Woodstock, VT: Jewish Lights, 2006.

Bernstein, Ellen, ed. *Ecology & the Jewish Spirit: Where Nature and the Sacred Meet.* Woodstock, VT: Jewish Lights, 2000.

Comins, Rabbi Michael. *A Wild Faith: Jewish Ways into Wilderness, Wilderness Ways into Judaism.* Woodstock, VT: Jewish Lights, 2007.

Isaacs, Ronald. *The Jewish Sourcebook on the Environment and Ecology.* Northvale, NJ: Jason Aronson Publishing, 1998.

Waskow, Rabbi Arthur, ed. *Torah of the Earth: Exploring 4,000 Years of Ecology in Jewish Thought.* 2 vols. Woodstock, VT: Jewish Lights, 2000.

Judaism and Healing

Brener, Anne. *Mourning & Mitzvah,* 2nd ed.: *A Guided Journal for Walking the Mourner's Path through Grief & Healing.* Woodstock, VT: Jewish Lights, 2001.

Cardin, Rabbi Nina Beth. *Tears of Sorrow, Seeds of Hope,* 2nd ed.: *A Jewish Spiritual Companion for Infertility and Pregnancy Loss.* Woodstock, VT: Jewish Lights, 1999.

Cutter, William ed. *Healing and the Jewish Imagination: Spiritual and Practical Perspectives on Judaism and Health.* Woodstock, VT: Jewish Lights, 2007.

Diamant, Anita. *Saying Kaddish: How to Comfort the Dying, Bury the Dead, and Mourn as a Jew.* New York: Schocken, 1998.

Olitzky, Kerry M. *Jewish Paths toward Healing and Wholeness: A Personal Guide to Dealing with Suffering.* Woodstock, VT: Jewish Lights, 2000.

Wieseltier, Leon. *Kaddish.* New York: Alfred A. Knopf. 1998.

Opening Doors to Judaism

The Way Into... Series offers a multi-volume, multi-author "guided tour" of the Jewish faith, people, history, and beliefs—in total, an accessible introduction to Judaism.

Multi-authors. *The Way Into...* Series. Woodstock, VT: Jewish Lights, 2000–.

Elkins, Dov Peretz. *The Wisdom of Judaism: An Introduction to the Values of the Talmud.* Woodstock, VT: Jewish Lights, 2007.

Hendler, Lee Meyerhoff. *The Year Mom Got Religion: One Woman's Midlife Journey into Judaism.* Woodstock, VT: Jewish Lights, 1999.

Kushner, Harold. *To Life! A Celebration of Jewish Being and Thinking*. Boston: Little, Brown, 1993.

Shapiro, Rami. *Ethics of the Sages:* Pirke Avot—*Annotated & Explained*. Woodstock, VT: SkyLight Paths, 2006.

Telushkin, Joseph. *Jewish Literacy: The Most Important Things to Know about the Jewish Religion, Its People, and Its History*. New York: William Morrow, 1991.

Social Justice

Rose, Or N., Jo Ellen Green Kaiser and Margie Klein, eds. *Righteous Indignation: A Jewish Call for Justice*. Woodstock, VT: Jewish Lights, 2007.

Sacks, Jonathan. *To Heal a Fractured World: The Ethics of Responsibility*. New York: Schocken Books, 2005.

Schwarz, Sidney. *Judaism and Justice: The Jewish Passion to Repair the World*. Woodstock, VT: Jewish Lights, 2006.

Spiritual Journeys

Dubner, Steven J. *Turbulent Souls: A Catholic Son's Return to His Jewish Family*. New York: William Morrow, 1998.

Firestone, Tirzah. *With Roots in Heaven: One Woman's Passionate Journey into the Heart of Her Faith*. New York: Plume, 1998.

Fuchs-Kreimer, Nancy. *Parenting as a Spiritual Journey: Deepening Ordinary & Extraordinary Events into Sacred Occasions*. Woodstock, VT: Jewish Lights, 1996.

Kamenetz, Rodger. *The Jew in the Lotus: A Poet's Rediscovery of Jewish Identity in Buddhist India*. New York: HarperCollins, 1994.

———. *Stalking Elijah: Adventures with Today's Jewish Mystical Masters*. San Francisco: HarperSan Francisco, 1997.

Pogrebin, Letty Cottin. *Deborah, Golda, and Me: Being Female and Jewish in America*. New York: Crown Publishers, 1991.

Women's Interest

Kates, Judith A. and Gail Twersky Reimer, eds. *Reading Ruth: Contemporary Women Reclaim a Sacred Story*. New York: Ballentine Books, 1994.

Plaskow, Judith. *Standing Again at Sinai: Judaism from a Feminist Perspective*. New York: HarperCollins, 1990.

Umansky, Ellen M. and Dianne Aston, eds. *Four Centuries of Jewish Women's Spirituality: A Sourcebook*. Boston: Beacon Press, 1992.

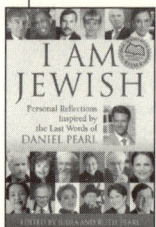

I Am Jewish
Personal Reflections Inspired by the Last Words of Daniel Pearl
Almost 150 Jews—both famous and not—from all walks of life, from all around the world, write about Identity, Heritage, Covenant / Chosenness and Faith, Humanity and Ethnicity, and *Tikkun Olam* and Justice.
Edited by Judea and Ruth Pearl
6 x 9, 304 pp, Deluxe PB w/flaps, 978-1-58023-259-3 **$18.99**
Download a free copy of the *I Am Jewish Teacher's Guide* at our website: www.jewishlights.com

Children's Books

What You Will See Inside a Synagogue
By Rabbi Lawrence A. Hoffman and Dr. Ron Wolfson; Full-color photos by Bill Aron
A colorful, fun-to-read introduction that explains the ways and whys of Jewish worship and religious life.
8½ x 10½, 32 pp, Full-color photos, HC, 978-1-59473-012-2 **$17.99** *For ages 6 & up (A SkyLight Paths book)*

The Kids' Fun Book of Jewish Time
By Emily Sper 9 x 7½, 24 pp, Full-color illus., HC, 978-1-58023-311-8 **$16.99**

In God's Hands
By Lawrence Kushner and Gary Schmidt 9 x 12, 32 pp, HC, 978-1-58023-224-1 **$16.99**

Because Nothing Looks Like God
By Lawrence and Karen Kushner
Introduces children to the possibilities of spiritual life.
11 x 8½, 32 pp, Full-color illus., HC, 978-1-58023-092-6 **$16.95** *For ages 4 & up*

Also Available: **Because Nothing Looks Like God Teacher's Guide**
8½ x 11, 22 pp, PB, 978-1-58023-140-4 **$6.95** *For ages 5–8*

Board Book Companions to *Because Nothing Looks Like God*
5 x 5, 24 pp, Full-color illus., SkyLight Paths Board Books *For ages 0–4*

What Does God Look Like? 978-1-893361-23-2 **$7.99**

How Does God Make Things Happen? 978-1-893361-24-9 **$7.95**

Where Is God? 978-1-893361-17-1 **$7.99**

The Book of Miracles: A Young Person's Guide to Jewish Spiritual Awareness
By Lawrence Kushner. All-new illustrations by the author
6 x 9, 96 pp, 2-color illus., HC, 978-1-879045-78-1 **$16.95** *For ages 9 and up*

In Our Image: God's First Creatures
By Nancy Sohn Swartz 9 x 12, 32 pp, Full-color illus., HC, 978-1-879045-99-6 **$16.95** *For ages 4 & up*

Also Available as a Board Book: **How Did the Animals Help God?**
5 x 5, 24 pp, Board, Full-color illus., 978-1-59473-044-3 **$7.99** *For ages 0–4 (A SkyLight Paths book)*

What Makes Someone a Jew?
By Lauren Seidman
Reflects the changing face of American Judaism.
10 x 8½, 32 pp, Full-color photos, Quality PB Original, 978-1-58023-321-7 **$8.99** *For ages 3–6*

Or phone, fax, mail or e-mail to: **JEWISH LIGHTS** Publishing
Sunset Farm Offices, Route 4 • P.O. Box 237 • Woodstock, Vermont 05091
Tel: (802) 457-4000 • Fax: (802) 457-4004 • www.jewishlights.com
Credit card orders: **(800) 962-4544** (8:30AM–5:30PM ET Monday–Friday)
Generous discounts on quantity orders. SATISFACTION GUARANTEED. Prices subject to change.

Meditation

The Handbook of Jewish Meditation Practices
A Guide for Enriching the Sabbath and Other Days of Your Life
By Rabbi David A. Cooper Easy-to-learn meditation techniques.
6 x 9, 208 pp, Quality PB, 978-1-58023-102-2 **$16.95**

Discovering Jewish Meditation: Instruction & Guidance for Learning an Ancient
Spiritual Practice *By Nan Fink Gefen*
6 x 9, 208 pp, Quality PB, 978-1-58023-067-4 **$16.95**

A Heart of Stillness: A Complete Guide to Learning the Art of Meditation
By David A. Cooper 5½ x 8½, 272 pp, Quality PB, 978-1-893361-03-4 **$16.95** *(A SkyLight Paths book)*

Meditation from the Heart of Judaism: Today's Teachers Share Their
Practices, Techniques, and Faith *Edited by Avram Davis*
6 x 9, 256 pp, Quality PB, 978-1-58023-049-0 **$16.95**

Silence, Simplicity & Solitude: A Complete Guide to Spiritual Retreat at Home
By David A. Cooper 5½ x 8½, 336 pp, Quality PB, 978-1-893361-04-1 **$16.95**
(A SkyLight Paths book)

The Way of Flame: A Guide to the Forgotten Mystical Tradition of Jewish
Meditation *By Avram Davis* 4½ x 8, 176 pp, Quality PB, 978-1-58023-060-5 **$15.95**

Ritual/Sacred Practice/Journaling

The Jewish Dream Book: The Key to Opening the Inner Meaning of
Your Dreams *By Vanessa L. Ochs with Elizabeth Ochs; Full-color illus. by Kristina Swarner*
Instructions for how modern people can perform ancient Jewish dream practices
and dream interpretations drawn from the Jewish wisdom tradition.
8 x 8, 128 pp, Full-color illus., Deluxe PB w/flaps, 978-1-58023-132-9 **$16.95**

The Jewish Journaling Book: How to Use Jewish Tradition to Write
Your Life & Explore Your Soul *By Janet Ruth Falon*
Details the history of Jewish journaling throughout biblical and modern times, and
teaches specific journaling techniques to help you create and maintain a vital journal,
from a Jewish perspective. 8 x 8, 304 pp, Deluxe PB w/flaps, 978-1-58023-203-6 **$18.99**

The Book of Jewish Sacred Practices: CLAL's Guide to Everyday & Holiday
Rituals & Blessings *Edited by Rabbi Irwin Kula and Vanessa L. Ochs, PhD*
6 x 9, 368 pp, Quality PB, 978-1-58023-152-7 **$18.95**

Jewish Ritual: A Brief Introduction for Christians
By Rabbi Kerry M. Olitzky and Rabbi Daniel Judson
5½ x 8½, 144 pp, Quality PB, 978-1-58023-210-4 **$14.99**

The Rituals & Practices of a Jewish Life: A Handbook for Personal Spiritual
Renewal *Edited by Rabbi Kerry M. Olitzky and Rabbi Daniel Judson*
6 x 9, 272 pp, illus., Quality PB, 978-1-58023-169-5 **$18.95**

The Sacred Art of Lovingkindness: Preparing to Practice
By Rabbi Rami Shapiro 5½ x 8½, 176 pp, Quality PB, 978-1-59473-151-8 **$16.99**
(A SkyLight Paths book)

Science Fiction/Mystery & Detective Fiction

Mystery Midrash: An Anthology of Jewish Mystery & Detective Fiction
Edited by Lawrence W. Raphael; Preface by Joel Siegel
6 x 9, 304 pp, Quality PB, 978-1-58023-055-1 **$16.95**

Criminal Kabbalah: An Intriguing Anthology of Jewish Mystery & Detective Fiction
Edited by Lawrence W. Raphael; Foreword by Laurie R. King
6 x 9, 256 pp, Quality PB, 978-1-58023-109-1 **$16.95**

Wandering Stars: An Anthology of Jewish Fantasy & Science Fiction
Edited by Jack Dann; Introduction by Isaac Asimov
6 x 9, 272 pp, Quality PB, 978-1-58023-005-6 **$16.95**

More Wandering Stars: An Anthology of Outstanding Stories of Jewish Fantasy and
Science Fiction *Edited by Jack Dann; Introduction by Isaac Asimov*
6 x 9, 192 pp, Quality PB, 978-1-58023-063-6 **$16.95**

Inspiration

God's To-Do List: 103 Ways to Be an Angel and Do God's Work on Earth
By Dr. Ron Wolfson 6 x 9, 150 pp, Quality PB, 978-1-58023-301-9 **$15.99**

God in All Moments: Mystical & Practical Spiritual Wisdom from Hasidic Masters
Edited and translated by Or N. Rose with Ebn D. Leader
5½ x 8½, 192 pp, Quality PB, 978-1-58023-186-2 **$16.95**

Our Dance with God: Finding Prayer, Perspective and Meaning in the Stories of Our
Lives *By Karyn D. Kedar* 6 x 9, 176 pp, Quality PB, 978-1-58023-202-9 **$16.99**

Also Available: **The Dance of the Dolphin** (HC edition of *Our Dance with God*)
6 x 9, 176 pp, HC, 978-1-58023-154-1 **$19.95**

The Empty Chair: Finding Hope and Joy—Timeless Wisdom from a Hasidic Master,
Rebbe Nachman of Breslov *Adapted by Moshe Mykoff and the Breslov Research Institute*
4 x 6, 128 pp, 2-color text, Deluxe PB w/flaps, 978-1-879045-67-5 **$9.95**

The Gentle Weapon: Prayers for Everyday and Not-So-Everyday Moments—
Timeless Wisdom from the Teachings of the Hasidic Master, Rebbe Nachman of Breslov
Adapted by Moshe Mykoff and S. C. Mizrahi, together with the Breslov Research Institute
4 x 6, 144 pp, 2-color text, Deluxe PB w/flaps, 978-1-58023-022-3 **$9.99**

God Whispers: Stories of the Soul, Lessons of the Heart *By Karyn D. Kedar*
6 x 9, 176 pp, Quality PB, 978-1-58023-088-9 **$15.95**

An Orphan in History: One Man's Triumphant Search for His Jewish Roots
By Paul Cowan; Afterword by Rachel Cowan. 6 x 9, 288 pp, Quality PB, 978-1-58023-135-0 **$16.95**

Restful Reflections: Nighttime Inspiration to Calm the Soul, Based on Jewish Wisdom
By Rabbi Kerry M. Olitzky & Rabbi Lori Forman 4½ x 6½, 448 pp, Quality PB, 978-1-58023-091-9 **$15.95**

Sacred Intentions: Daily Inspiration to Strengthen the Spirit, Based on Jewish Wisdom
By Rabbi Kerry M. Olitzky and Rabbi Lori Forman 4½ x 6½, 448 pp, Quality PB, 978-1-58023-061-2 **$15.95**

Kabbalah/Mysticism/Enneagram

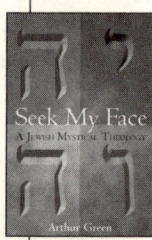

Awakening to Kabbalah: The Guiding Light of Spiritual Fulfillment
By Rav Michael Laitman, PhD 6 x 9, 192 pp, HC, 978-1-58023-264-7 **$21.99**

Seek My Face: A Jewish Mystical Theology *By Arthur Green*
6 x 9, 304 pp, Quality PB, 978-1-58023-130-5 **$19.95**

Zohar: Annotated & Explained
Translation and annotation by Daniel C. Matt; Foreword by Andrew Harvey
5½ x 8½, 176 pp, Quality PB, 978-1-893361-51-5 **$15.99** (A SkyLight Paths book)

Cast in God's Image: Discover Your Personality Type Using the Enneagram and Kabbalah
By Rabbi Howard A. Addison
7 x 9, 176 pp, Quality PB, Layflat binding, 20+ journaling exercises, 978-1-58023-124-4 **$16.95**

Ehyeh: A Kabbalah for Tomorrow
By Arthur Green 6 x 9, 224 pp, Quality PB, 978-1-58023-213-5 **$16.99**

The Enneagram and Kabbalah, 2nd Edition: Reading Your Soul
By Rabbi Howard A. Addison 6 x 9, 192 pp, Quality PB, 978-1-58023-229-6 **$16.99**

Finding Joy: A Practical Spiritual Guide to Happiness *By Dannel I. Schwartz with Mark Hass*
6 x 9, 192 pp, Quality PB, 978-1-58023-009-4 **$14.95**

The Flame of the Heart: Prayers of a Chasidic Mystic *By Reb Noson of Breslov. Translated by*
David Sears with the Breslov Research Institute 5 x 7¼, 160 pp, Quality PB, 978-1-58023-246-3 **$15.99**

The Gift of Kabbalah: Discovering the Secrets of Heaven, Renewing Your Life on Earth
By Tamar Frankiel, PhD 6 x 9, 256 pp, Quality PB, 978-1-58023-141-1 **$16.95;**
HC, 978-1-58023-108-4 **$21.95**

Kabbalah: A Brief Introduction for Christians
By Tamar Frankiel, PhD 5½ x 8½, 208 pp, Quality PB, 978-1-58023-303-3 **$16.99**

The Lost Princess and Other Kabbalistic Tales of Rebbe Nachman of Breslov
The Seven Beggars and Other Kabbalistic Tales of Rebbe Nachman of Breslov
Translated by Rabbi Aryeh Kaplan; Preface by Rabbi Chaim Kramer
Lost Princess: 6 x 9, 400 pp, Quality PB, 978-1-58023-217-3 **$18.99**
Seven Beggars: 6 x 9, 192 pp, Quality PB, 978-1-58023-250-0 **$16.99**

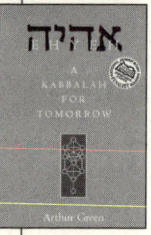

Current Events/History

The Story of the Jews: A 4,000-Year Adventure—A Graphic History Book
Written & illustrated by Stan Mack
Witty, illustrated narrative of all the major happenings from biblical times to the twenty-first century. 6 x 9, 288 pp, illus., Quality PB, 978-1-58023-155-8 **$16.95**

Hannah Senesh: Her Life and Diary, the First Complete Edition
By Hannah Senesh; Foreword by Marge Piercy; Preface by Eitan Senesh
6 x 9, 352 pp, HC, 978-1-58023-212-8 **$24.99**

The Jewish Prophet: Visionary Words from Moses and Miriam to Henrietta Szold and A. J. Heschel *By Rabbi Dr. Michael J. Shire*
6½ x 8½, 128 pp, 123 full-color illus., HC, 978-1-58023-168-8
Special gift price $14.95

Foundations of Sephardic Spirituality: The Inner Life of Jews of the Ottoman Empire
By Rabbi Marc D. Angel, PhD 6 x 9, 224 pp, HC, 978-1-58023-243-2 **$24.99**

Judaism and Justice: The Jewish Passion to Repair the World
By Rabbi Sidney Schwarz
6 x 9, 250 pp, HC, 978-1-58023-312-5 **$24.99**

Ecology

Ecology & the Jewish Spirit: Where Nature & the Sacred Meet
Edited by Ellen Bernstein 6 x 9, 288 pp, Quality PB, 978-1-58023-082-7 **$16.95**

Torah of the Earth: Exploring 4,000 Years of Ecology in Jewish Thought
Vol. 1: Biblical Israel: One Land, One People; Rabbinic Judaism: One People, Many Lands
Vol. 2: Zionism: One Land, Two Peoples; Eco-Judaism: One Earth, Many Peoples
Edited by Arthur Waskow
Vol. 1: 6 x 9, 272 pp, Quality PB, 978-1-58023-086-5 **$19.95**
Vol. 2: 6 x 9, 336 pp, Quality PB, 978-1-58023-087-2 **$19.95**

The Way Into Judaism and the Environment
By Jeremy Benstein 6 x 9, 224 pp, HC, 978-1-58023-268-5 **$24.99**

Grief/Healing

Against the Dying of the Light: A Parent's Story of Love, Loss and Hope
By Leonard Fein
5½ x 8½, 176 pp, Quality PB, 978-1-58023-197-8 **$15.99**

Grief in Our Seasons: A Mourner's Kaddish Companion *By Rabbi Kerry M. Olitzky*
4½ x 6½, 448 pp, Quality PB, 978-1-879045-55-2 **$15.95**

Healing of Soul, Healing of Body: Spiritual Leaders Unfold the Strength & Solace in Psalms *Edited by Rabbi Simkha Y. Weintraub, CSW*
6 x 9, 128 pp, 2-color illus. text, Quality PB, 978-1-879045-31-6 **$14.99**

Jewish Paths toward Healing and Wholeness: A Personal Guide to Dealing with Suffering *By Rabbi Kerry M. Olitzky; Foreword by Debbie Friedman.*
6 x 9, 192 pp, Quality PB, 978-1-58023-068-1 **$15.95**

Mourning & Mitzvah, 2nd Edition: A Guided Journal for Walking the Mourner's Path through Grief to Healing *By Anne Brener, LCSW*
7½ x 9, 304 pp, Quality PB, 978-1-58023-113-8 **$19.99**

The Perfect Stranger's Guide to Funerals and Grieving Practices
A Guide to Etiquette in Other People's Religious Ceremonies *Edited by Stuart M. Matlins*
6 x 9, 240 pp, Quality PB, 978-1-893361-20-1 **$16.95** *(A SkyLight Paths book)*

Tears of Sorrow, Seeds of Hope, 2nd Edition: A Jewish Spiritual Companion for Infertility and Pregnancy Loss *By Rabbi Nina Beth Cardin*
6 x 9, 208 pp, Quality PB, 978-1-58023-233-3 **$18.99**

A Time to Mourn, A Time to Comfort, 2nd Edition: A Guide to Jewish Bereavement *By Dr. Ron Wolfson*
7 x 9, 384 pp, Quality PB, 978-1-58023-253-1 **$19.99**

When a Grandparent Dies: A Kid's Own Remembering Workbook for Dealing with Shiva and the Year Beyond *By Nechama Liss-Levinson, PhD*
8 x 10, 48 pp, 2-color text, HC, 978-1-879045-44-6 **$15.95** *For ages 7–13*

Holidays/Holy Days

Rosh Hashanah Readings: Inspiration, Information and Contemplation
Yom Kippur Readings: Inspiration, Information and Contemplation
Edited by Rabbi Dov Peretz Elkins with Section Introductions from Arthur Green's These Are the Words
An extraordinary collection of readings, prayers and insights that enable the modern worshiper to enter into the spirit of the High Holy Days in a personal and powerful way, permitting the meaning of the Jewish New Year to enter the heart.
RHR: 6 x 9, 400 pp, HC, 978-1-58023-239-5 **$24.99**
YKR: 6 x 9, 368 pp, HC, 978-1-58023-271-5 **$24.99**

Jewish Holidays: A Brief Introduction for Christians
By Rabbi Kerry M. Olitzky and Rabbi Daniel Judson
5½ x 8½, 144 pp, Quality PB, 978-1-58023-302-6 **$16.99**

Leading the Passover Journey: The Seder's Meaning Revealed, the Haggadah's Story Retold *By Rabbi Nathan Laufer*
Uncovers the hidden meaning of the Seder's rituals and customs.
6 x 9, 224 pp, HC, 978-1-58023-211-1 **$24.99**

Reclaiming Judaism as a Spiritual Practice: Holy Days and Shabbat
By Rabbi Goldie Milgram
7 x 9, 272 pp, Quality PB, 978-1-58023-205-0 **$19.99**

7th Heaven: Celebrating Shabbat with Rebbe Nachman of Breslov
By Moshe Mykoff with the Breslov Research Institute
5⅛ x 8¼, 224 pp, Deluxe PB w/flaps, 978-1-58023-175-6 **$18.95**

The Women's Passover Companion: Women's Reflections on the Festival of Freedom *Edited by Rabbi Sharon Cohen Anisfeld, Tara Mohr, and Catherine Spector*
Groundbreaking. A provocative conversation about women's relationships to Passover as well as the roots and meanings of women's seders.
6 x 9, 352 pp, Quality PB, 978-1-58023-231-9 **$19.99**

The Women's Seder Sourcebook: Rituals & Readings for Use at the Passover Seder *Edited by Rabbi Sharon Cohen Anisfeld, Tara Mohr, and Catherine Spector*
Gathers the voices of more than one hundred women in readings, personal and creative reflections, commentaries, blessings, and ritual suggestions that can be incorporated into your Passover celebration.
6 x 9, 384 pp, Quality PB, 978-1-58023-232-6 **$19.99**

Creating Lively Passover Seders: A Sourcebook of Engaging Tales, Texts & Activities
By David Arnow, PhD 7 x 9, 416 pp, Quality PB, 978-1-58023-184-8 **$24.99**

Hanukkah, 2nd Edition: The Family Guide to Spiritual Celebration
By Dr. Ron Wolfson. Edited by Joel Lurie Grishaver.
7 x 9, 240 pp, illus., Quality PB, 978-1-58023-122-0 **$18.95**

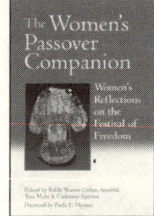

The Jewish Family Fun Book: Holiday Projects, Everyday Activities, and Travel Ideas
with Jewish Themes *By Danielle Dardashti and Roni Sarig. Illus. by Avi Katz.*
6 x 9, 288 pp, 70+ b/w illus. & diagrams, Quality PB, 978-1-58023-171-8 **$18.95**

The Jewish Gardening Cookbook: Growing Plants & Cooking for Holidays
& Festivals *By Michael Brown* 6 x 9, 224 pp, 30+ b/w illus., Quality PB, 978-1-58023-116-9 **$16.95**

The Jewish Lights Book of Fun Classroom Activities: Simple and Seasonal
Projects for Teachers and Students *By Danielle Dardashti and Roni Sarig*
6 x 9, 240 pp, Quality PB, 978-1-58023-206-7 **$19.99**

Passover, 2nd Edition: The Family Guide to Spiritual Celebration
By Dr. Ron Wolfson with Joel Lurie Grishaver 7 x 9, 352 pp, Quality PB, 978-1-58023-174-9 **$19.95**

Shabbat, 2nd Edition: The Family Guide to Preparing for and Celebrating the Sabbath
By Dr. Ron Wolfson 7 x 9, 320 pp, illus., Quality PB, 978-1-58023-164-0 **$19.99**

Sharing Blessings: Children's Stories for Exploring the Spirit of the Jewish Holidays
By Rahel Musleah and Rabbi Michael Klayman
8½ x 11, 64 pp, Full-color illus., HC, 978-1-879045-71-2 **$18.95** *For ages 6 & up*

Life Cycle
Marriage / Parenting / Family / Aging

Jewish Fathers: A Legacy of Love
Photographs by Lloyd Wolf. Essays by Paula Wolfson. Foreword by Rabbi Harold Kushner.
Honors the role of contemporary Jewish fathers in America. Each father tells in his own words what it means to be a parent and Jewish, and what he learned from his own father. Insightful photos.
10¾ x 9⅞, 144 pp with 100+ duotone photos, HC, 978-1-58023-204-3 **$30.00**

The New Jewish Baby Album: Creating and Celebrating the Beginning of a Spiritual Life—A Jewish Lights Companion
By the Editors at Jewish Lights. Foreword by Anita Diamant. Preface by Rabbi Sandy Eisenberg Sasso.
A spiritual keepsake that will be treasured for generations. More than just a memory book, *shows you how—and why it's important*—to create a Jewish home and a Jewish life. 8 x 10, 64 pp, Deluxe Padded HC, Full-color illus., 978-1-58023-138-1 **$19.95**

The Jewish Pregnancy Book: A Resource for the Soul, Body & Mind during Pregnancy, Birth & the First Three Months
By Sandy Falk, MD, and Rabbi Daniel Judson, with Steven A. Rapp
Includes medical information, prayers and rituals for each stage of pregnancy, from a liberal Jewish perspective. 7 x 10, 208 pp, Quality PB, b/w photos, 978-1-58023-178-7 **$16.95**

Celebrating Your New Jewish Daughter: Creating Jewish Ways to Welcome Baby Girls into the Covenant—New and Traditional Ceremonies *By Debra Nussbaum Cohen; Foreword by Rabbi Sandy Eisenberg Sasso* 6 x 9, 272 pp, Quality PB, 978-1-58023-090-2 **$18.95**

The New Jewish Baby Book, 2nd Edition: Names, Ceremonies & Customs—A Guide for Today's Families *By Anita Diamant* 6 x 9, 336 pp, Quality PB, 978-1-58023-251-7 **$19.99**

Parenting As a Spiritual Journey: Deepening Ordinary and Extraordinary Events into Sacred Occasions *By Rabbi Nancy Fuchs-Kreimer*
6 x 9, 224 pp, Quality PB, 978-1-58023-016-2 **$16.95**

Parenting Jewish Teens: A Guide for the Perplexed
By Joanne Doades 6 x 9, 200 pp, Quality PB, 978-1-58023-305-7 **$16.99**

Judaism for Two: A Spiritual Guide for Strengthening and Celebrating Your Loving Relationship *By Rabbi Nancy Fuchs-Kreimer and Rabbi Nancy H. Wiener; Foreword by Rabbi Elliot N. Dorff* Addresses the ways Jewish teachings can enhance and strengthen committed relationships. 6 x 9, 224 pp, Quality PB, 978-1-58023-254-8 **$16.99**

Embracing the Covenant: Converts to Judaism Talk About Why & How
By Rabbi Allan Berkowitz and Patti Moskovitz 6 x 9, 192 pp, Quality PB, 978-1-879045-50-7 **$16.95**

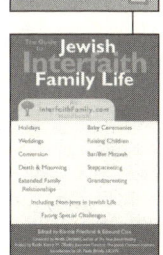

The Guide to Jewish Interfaith Family Life: An InterfaithFamily.com Handbook
Edited by Ronnie Friedland and Edmund Case 6 x 9, 384 pp, Quality PB, 978-1-58023-153-4 **$18.95**

Introducing My Faith and My Community
The Jewish Outreach Institute Guide for the Christian in a Jewish Interfaith Relationship
By Rabbi Kerry M. Olitzky 6 x 9, 176 pp, Quality PB, 978-1-58023-192-3 **$16.99**

Making a Successful Jewish Interfaith Marriage: The Jewish Outreach Institute Guide to Opportunities, Challenges and Resources *By Rabbi Kerry M. Olitzky with Joan Peterson Littman*
6 x 9, 176 pp, Quality PB, 978-1-58023-170-1 **$16.95**

The Creative Jewish Wedding Book: A Hands-On Guide to New & Old Traditions, Ceremonies & Celebrations *By Gabrielle Kaplan-Mayer*
9 x 9, 288 pp, b/w photos, Quality PB, 978-1-58023-194-7 **$19.99**

Divorce Is a Mitzvah: A Practical Guide to Finding Wholeness and Holiness When Your Marriage Dies *By Rabbi Perry Netter; Afterword by Rabbi Laura Geller.*
6 x 9, 224 pp, Quality PB, 978-1-58023-172-5 **$16.95**

A Heart of Wisdom: Making the Jewish Journey from Midlife through the Elder Years
Edited by Susan Berrin; Foreword by Harold Kushner
6 x 9, 384 pp, Quality PB, 978-1-58023-051-3 **$18.95**

So That Your Values Live On: Ethical Wills and How to Prepare Them
Edited by Jack Riemer and Nathaniel Stampfer
6 x 9, 272 pp, Quality PB, 978-1-879045-34-7 **$18.99**

Spirituality

The Adventures of Rabbi Harvey: A Graphic Novel of Jewish Wisdom and Wit in the Wild West *By Steve Sheinkin*
Jewish and American folktales combine in this witty and original graphic novel collection. Creatively retold and set on the western frontier of the 1870s.
6 x 9, 144 pp, Full-color illus., Quality PB, 978-1-58023-310-1 **$16.99**
Also Available: **The Adventures of Rabbi Harvey Teacher's Guide**
8½ x 11, 32 pp, PB, 978-1-58023-326-2 **$8.99**

Ethics of the Sages: *Pirke Avot*—Annotated & Explained
Translation and Annotation by Rabbi Rami Shapiro
5½ x 8½, 192 pp, Quality PB, 978-1-59473-207-2 **$16.99** *(A SkyLight Paths book)*

A Book of Life: Embracing Judaism as a Spiritual Practice
By Michael Strassfeld 6 x 9, 528 pp, Quality PB, 978-1-58023-247-0 **$19.99**

Meaning and Mitzvah: Daily Practices for Reclaiming Judaism through Prayer, God, Torah, Hebrew, Mitzvot and Peoplehood *By Rabbi Goldie Milgram*
7 x 9, 336 pp, Quality PB, 978-1-58023-256-2 **$19.99**

The Soul of the Story: Meetings with Remarkable People
By Rabbi David Zeller 6 x 9, 288 pp, HC, 978-1-58023-272-2 **$21.99**

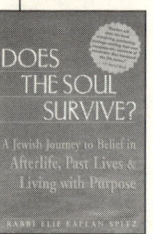

Aleph-Bet Yoga: Embodying the Hebrew Letters for Physical and Spiritual Well-Being
By Steven A. Rapp. Foreword by Tamar Frankiel, PhD and Judy Greenfeld. Preface by Hart Lazer.
7 x 10, 128 pp, b/w photos, Quality PB, Layflat binding, 978-1-58023-162-6 **$16.95**

Entering the Temple of Dreams: Jewish Prayers, Movements, and Meditations for the End of the Day *By Tamar Frankiel, PhD, and Judy Greenfeld*
7 x 10, 192 pp, illus., Quality PB, 978-1-58023-079-7 **$16.95**

Does the Soul Survive? A Jewish Journey to Belief in Afterlife, Past Lives & Living with Purpose *By Rabbi Elie Kaplan Spitz; Foreword by Brian L. Weiss, MD*
6 x 9, 288 pp, Quality PB, 978-1-58023-165-7 **$16.99**

First Steps to a New Jewish Spirit: Reb Zalman's Guide to Recapturing the Intimacy & Ecstasy in Your Relationship with God *By Rabbi Zalman M. Schachter-Shalomi with Donald Gropman* 6 x 9, 144 pp, Quality PB, 978-1-58023-182-4 **$16.95**

God in Our Relationships: Spirituality between People from the Teachings of Martin Buber *By Rabbi Dennis S. Ross* 5½ x 8½, 160 pp, Quality PB, 978-1-58023-147-3 **$16.95**

Judaism, Physics and God: Searching for Sacred Metaphors in a Post-Einstein World
By Rabbi David W. Nelson 6 x 9, 368 pp, Quality PB, inc. reader's discussion guide, 978-1-58023-306-4 **$18.99**;
HC, 352 pp, 978-1-58023-252-4 **$24.99**

The Jewish Lights Spirituality Handbook: A Guide to Understanding, Exploring & Living a Spiritual Life *Edited by Stuart M. Matlins*
What exactly is "Jewish" about spirituality? How do I make it a part of my life? Fifty of today's foremost spiritual leaders share their ideas and experience with us.
6 x 9, 456 pp, Quality PB, 978-1-58023-093-3 **$19.99**

Bringing the Psalms to Life: How to Understand and Use the Book of Psalms
By Daniel F. Polish 6 x 9, 208 pp, Quality PB, 978-1-58023-157-2 **$16.95**;
HC, 978-1-58023-077-3 **$21.95**

God & the Big Bang: Discovering Harmony between Science & Spirituality
By Daniel C. Matt 6 x 9, 216 pp, Quality PB, 978-1-879045-89-7 **$16.99**

Minding the Temple of the Soul: Balancing Body, Mind, and Spirit through Traditional Jewish Prayer, Movement, and Meditation *By Tamar Frankiel, PhD, and Judy Greenfeld*
7 x 10, 184 pp, illus., Quality PB, 978-1-879045-64-4 **$16.95**
Audiotape of the Blessings and Meditations: 60 min. **$9.95**
Videotape of the Movements and Meditations: 46 min. **$20.00**

One God Clapping: The Spiritual Path of a Zen Rabbi *By Alan Lew with Sherril Jaffe*
5½ x 8½, 336 pp, Quality PB, 978-1-58023-115-2 **$16.95**

There Is No Messiah ... and You're It: The Stunning Transformation of Judaism's Most Provocative Idea *By Rabbi Robert N. Levine, DD*
6 x 9, 192 pp, Quality PB, 978-1-58023-255-5 **$16.99**

These Are the Words: A Vocabulary of Jewish Spiritual Life
By Arthur Green 6 x 9, 304 pp, Quality PB, 978-1-58023-107-7 **$18.95**

Spirituality/Women's Interest

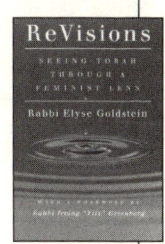

The Quotable Jewish Woman: Wisdom, Inspiration & Humor from the Mind & Heart
Edited and compiled by Elaine Bernstein Partnow
6 x 9, 496 pp, Quality PB, 978-1-58023-236-4 **$19.99**; HC, 978-1-58023-193-0 **$29.99**

The Knitting Way: A Guide to Spiritual Self-Discovery *By Linda Skolnick and Janice MacDaniels* 7 x 9, 240 pp, Quality PB, 978-1-59473-079-5 **$16.99** *(A SkyLight Paths book)*

The Quilting Path: A Guide to Spiritual Self-Discovery through Fabric, Thread and Kabbalah
By Louise Silk 7 x 9, 192 pp, Quality PB, 978-1-59473-206-5 **$16.99** *(A SkyLight Paths book)*

The Divine Feminine in Biblical Wisdom Literature: Selections Annotated &
Explained *Translated and Annotated by Rabbi Rami Shapiro*
5½ x 8½, 240 pp, Quality PB, 978-1-59473-109-9 **$16.99** *(A SkyLight Paths book)*

Lifecycles, Vol. 1: Jewish Women on Life Passages & Personal Milestones
Edited and with Introductions by Rabbi Debra Orenstein
6 x 9, 480 pp, Quality PB, 978-1-58023-018-2 **$19.95**

Lifecycles, Vol. 2: Jewish Women on Biblical Themes in Contemporary Life
Edited and with Introductions by Rabbi Debra Orenstein and Rabbi Jane Rachel Litman
6 x 9, 464 pp, Quality PB, 978-1-58023-019-3 **$19.95**

Moonbeams: A Hadassah Rosh Hodesh Guide *Edited by Carol Diament, PhD*
8½ x 11, 240 pp, Quality PB, 978-1-58023-099-5 **$20.00**

ReVisions: Seeing Torah through a Feminist Lens *By Rabbi Elyse Goldstein*
5½ x 8½, 224 pp, Quality PB, 978-1-58023-117-6 **$16.95**

The Women's Haftarah Commentary: New Insights from Women Rabbis on the
54 Weekly Haftarah Portions, the 5 Megillot & Special Shabbatot
Edited by Rabbi Elyse Goldstein 6 x 9, 560 pp, HC, 978-1-58023-133-6 **$39.99**

The Women's Torah Commentary: New Insights from Women Rabbis on the 54
Weekly Torah Portions *Edited by Rabbi Elyse Goldstein*
6 x 9, 496 pp, HC, 978-1-58023-076-6 **$34.95**

The Year Mom Got Religion: One Woman's Midlife Journey into Judaism
By Lee Meyerhoff Hendler 6 x 9, 208 pp, Quality PB, 978-1-58023-070-4 **$15.95**

See Holidays for *The Women's Passover Companion: Women's Reflections on
the Festival of Freedom* and *The Women's Seder Sourcebook: Rituals &
Readings for Use at the Passover Seder.*

Travel

Israel—A Spiritual Travel Guide, 2nd Edition
A Companion for the Modern Jewish Pilgrim
By Rabbi Lawrence A. Hoffman 4¾ x 10, 256 pp, Quality PB, illus., 978-1-58023-261-6 **$18.99**
Also Available: **The Israel Mission Leader's Guide** 978-1-58023-085-8 **$4.95**

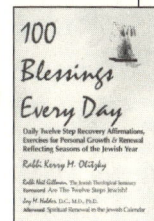

12-Step

100 Blessings Every Day: Daily Twelve Step Recovery Affirmations, Exercises for
Personal Growth & Renewal Reflecting Seasons of the Jewish Year
By Rabbi Kerry M. Olitzky; Foreword by Rabbi Neil Gillman
4½ x 6½, 432 pp, Quality PB, 978-1-879045-30-9 **$15.99**

Recovery from Codependence: A Jewish Twelve Steps Guide to Healing Your Soul
By Rabbi Kerry M. Olitzky 6 x 9, 160 pp, Quality PB, 978-1-879045-32-3 **$13.95**

Renewed Each Day: Daily Twelve Step Recovery Meditations Based on the Bible
By Rabbi Kerry M. Olitzky and Aaron Z.
Vol. 1—Genesis & Exodus: 6 x 9, 224 pp, Quality PB, 978-1-879045-12-5 **$14.95**
Vol. 2—Leviticus, Numbers & Deuteronomy: 6 x 9, 280 pp, Quality PB, 978-1-879045-13-2 **$18.99**

Twelve Jewish Steps to Recovery: A Personal Guide to Turning from Alcoholism &
Other Addictions—Drugs, Food, Gambling, Sex...
By Rabbi Kerry M. Olitzky and Stuart A. Copans, MD; Preface by Abraham J. Twerski, MD
6 x 9, 144 pp, Quality PB, 978-1-879045-09-5 **$14.95**

About Jewish Lights

People of all faiths and backgrounds yearn for books that attract, engage, educate, and spiritually inspire.

Our principal goal is to stimulate thought and help all people learn about who the Jewish People are, where they come from, and what the future can be made to hold. While people of our diverse Jewish heritage are the primary audience, our books speak to people in the Christian world as well and will broaden their understanding of Judaism and the roots of their own faith.

We bring to you authors who are at the forefront of spiritual thought and experience. While each has something different to say, they all say it in a voice that you can hear.

Our books are designed to welcome you and then to engage, stimulate, and inspire. We judge our success not only by whether or not our books are beautiful and commercially successful, but by whether or not they make a difference in your life.

For your information and convenience, at the back of this book we have provided a list of other Jewish Lights books you might find interesting and useful. They cover all the categories of your life:

Bar/Bat Mitzvah	Life Cycle
Bible Study / Midrash	Meditation
Children's Books	Parenting
Congregation Resources	Prayer
Current Events / History	Ritual / Sacred Practice
Ecology	Spirituality
Fiction: Mystery, Science Fiction	Theology / Philosophy
Grief / Healing	Travel
Holidays / Holy Days	12-Step
Inspiration	Women's Interest
Kabbalah / Mysticism / Enneagram	

Stuart M. Matlins, Publisher

Or phone, fax, mail or e-mail to: **JEWISH LIGHTS Publishing**
Sunset Farm Offices, Route 4 • P.O. Box 237 • Woodstock, Vermont 05091
Tel: (802) 457-4000 • Fax: (802) 457-4004 • www.jewishlights.com
Credit card orders: (800) 962-4544 (8:30AM–5:30PM ET Monday–Friday)
Generous discounts on quantity orders. SATISFACTION GUARANTEED. Prices subject to change.

For more information about each book, visit our website at www.jewishlights.com